Inventory of Amphibians and Reptiles at Fire Island National Seashore

Natural Resource Report NPS/NCBN/NRTR—2010/378

Robert P. Cook

National Park Service
Cape Cod National Seashore
Wellfleet, MA 02667
Robert_Cook@nps.gov

David K. Brotherton and John L. Behler[1]

Department of Herpetology
Wildlife Conservation Society
Bronx Zoo
Bronx, NY 10460-1099
dkb4112@yahoo.com
[1]deceased

September 2010

U.S. Department of the Interior
National Park Service
Natural Resource Program Center
Fort Collins, Colorado

The National Park Service, Natural Resource Program Center publishes a range of reports that address natural resource topics of interest and applicability to a broad audience in the National Park Service and others in natural resource management, including scientists, conservation and environmental constituencies, and the public.

The Natural Resource Technical Report Series is used to disseminate results of scientific studies in the physical, biological, and social sciences for both the advancement of science and the achievement of the National Park Service mission. The series provides contributors with a forum for displaying comprehensive data that are often deleted from journals because of page limitations.

All manuscripts in the series receive the appropriate level of peer review to ensure that the information is scientifically credible, technically accurate, appropriately written for the intended audience, and designed and published in a professional manner.

This report received informal peer review by subject-matter experts who were not directly involved in the collection, analysis, or reporting of the data. Data in this report were collected and analyzed using methods based on established, peer-reviewed protocols and were analyzed and interpreted within the guidelines of the protocols.

Views, statements, findings, conclusions, recommendations, and data in this report do not necessarily reflect views and policies of the National Park Service, U.S. Department of the Interior. Mention of trade names or commercial products does not constitute endorsement or recommendation for use by the U.S. Government.

This report is available from (http://www.nps.gov/nero/science/) and the Natural Resource Publications Management website (http://www.nature.nps.gov/publications/NRPM).

Please cite this publication as:

Cook, R. P., D. K. Brotherton, and J. L. Behler. 2010. Inventory of amphibians and reptiles at Fire Island National Seashore. Natural Resource Technical Report NPS/NCBN/NRTR—2010/378. National Park Service, Fort Collins, Colorado.

NPS 615/105745, September 2010

Contents

Figures

Tables

Appendices

Executive Summary

Under a National Park Service (NPS)/Wildlife Conservation Society Cooperative Agreement, we inventoried amphibians and reptiles on Fire Island National Seashore (FIIS) from March through September 2002, with additional turtle surveys in spring 2003. Six sampling methods were used; anuran calling surveys, visual encounter surveys, coverboards, turtle trap surveys, minnow trap surveys, and drift fencing. We also recorded animals encountered incidentally, including an eastern hog-nosed snake observed in 2007.

We recorded 12 species: 2 migrant and 10 resident. The 10 resident species represent 90% (9/10) of the species believed to have historically occurred on FIIS, plus a recent introduction, American bullfrog. These 12 species include two anurans, seven turtles, and three snakes. Fowler's toad, snapping turtle, and northern black racer were the most abundant and widely distributed species in each taxonomic group. "Listed" species recorded were the eastern mud turtle (NY *Endangered*)), eastern hog-nosed snake, spotted turtle, and eastern box turtle (NY *Special Concern*), and two migrant sea turtles, loggerhead (NY and federally *Threatened*) and leatherback (NY and federally *Endangered*), that washed up dead on the beach. Of the methods used, incidental encounter recorded 10 of 12 species, followed by visual encounter survey (7), turtle trap survey (5), drift fence (4), coverboard and minnow trap survey (2), and anuran calling survey (1). Eleven species were recorded in upland habitats and nine in wetland. By tract, the combined Watch Hill-OPWA tract has the greatest resident species richness, eight species, followed by the Lighthouse tract, with six species recorded.

Fire Island has relatively few species of amphibians and reptiles compared to "mainland" Long Island. The naturally-depauperate herpetofauna of FIIS is the result of geographic isolation, limited freshwater habitat, and harsh environmental conditions. Of the 10 resident species known to have occurred historically, seven appear stable in terms of population trend. Of the remaining three, Fowler's toad may be less common or at least underwent a decline in recent decades from which it has mostly recovered. The southern leopard frog has been extirpated and the eastern hog-nosed snake, last documented at FIIS in the 1970's, was not recorded in 2002 or 2003. However, an incidental observation by NPS staff in 2007 indicates it is present, but extremely rare. These three species have declined regionally, due to habitat loss and pesticide use. Their decline on FIIS is likely due partly to these factors, plus those natural factors noted above that limit recolonization. In spite of these limitations, FIIS is an important site, especially for reptiles, with four of the resident species present listed by New York State as either *Endangered* or *Special Concern*. Because many of the stressors that are negatively impacting these species regionally do not operate at FIIS, populations within the park are relatively well protected and FIIS plays an important role in helping to preserve the region's herpetofaunal diversity.

While a detailed plan for monitoring is beyond the scope of this inventory, the results suggest that a program based on anuran calling surveys, time or spatially constrained surveys, turtle trapping, and monitoring freshwater wetland water quality would be the most useful for generating quantitative data for trends analysis. Further work on eastern mud turtle, spotted turtle, eastern box turtle, and eastern-hog-nosed snake should be a high priority.

Acknowledgments

Funding for this project was provided by the National Park Service, and numerous people assisted with the project. Charlie Eichelberger and Linh Phu spent countless hours in the field at all hours of the day and night, organized and summarized the data gathered, and provided summaries of their findings. Steve Finn was especially helpful with providing information on the natural history of the park as well as identifying important wetland habitats likely to support amphibians and reptiles. Linda Gormenzano, Michael Bilecki, Bernie Felix, John Stewart, various parks rangers, and other National Park Service staff helped in many ways. Special thanks are extended to Norm Soule, director of Cold Spring Harbor Fish Hatchery, for guidance provided on mud turtle surveys, and to Jeremy Feinberg and Peter Warney for sharing their knowledge of the herpetofauna in and around Fire Island.

Preliminary drafts of this report were improved as a result of critical review and comments by Michael Bilecki and Dennis Skidds, who also provide GIS and map support. Special thanks to Robin Baranowski for final formatting.

Introduction

Fire Island National Seashore encompasses most of Fire Island, a barrier island located off the south shore of Long Island in Suffolk County, New York, approximately 89 km (55 miles) east of New York City. Recognized in the mid-20th century as a unique example of a still largely intact wilderness in close proximity to New York City (Murphy 1950), the park was established by Congress in 1964 to preserve the cultural and natural resources of Fire Island, its values of maritime and American history, barrier island dynamics and ecology, biodiversity, museum collections, and wilderness (NPS 2000). Fire Island provides habitat for a diversity of plant and wildlife species once more widely distributed along the coast of Long Island, including several species of Federal or New York State Endangered, Threatened, or Special Concern species. The William Floyd Estate, in nearby Mastic, Long Island is also administered by the National Park Service (NPS) as a unit of Fire Island National Seashore. However, because it is geographically distinct from Fire Island, the William Floyd Estate is treated separately and in this report Fire Island National Seashore (FIIS) refers only to lands on Fire Island.

In 1998, a Cooperative Agreement between the National Park Service and the Wildlife Conservation Society was established to assess amphibian and reptile populations at parks within the Northeast Region of the National Park Service. Although the goals of the project vary between parks, they generally are as follows:

- Assist the park service in documenting at least 90% of the species currently estimated to occur in the park.

- Determine the occurrence and status of species of management concern (e.g., state and federal *Threatened*, *Endangered*, and *Special Concern Species*, and other declining species).

- Determine abundance categories, distribution, and habitat use of documented species.

- Identify critical habitats of *Threatened*, *Endangered*, and *Special Concern* species.

- Provide basis for future development of a long term monitoring program.

- Analyze species occurrence against historical occurrence and evaluate the state of the park's herpetofauna, on a site and regional scale.

An "estimate" of species historically present at FIIS was generated using historical literature, NPS reports, and discussion with park staff. For the purpose of this "estimate", we differentiated between migratory species and resident species. Migratory species are the five species of marine turtles that occur with varying regularity in the western North Atlantic Ocean. These species nest far south of Fire Island and migrate north to feed as ocean temperatures increase in the summer. They occur in the open ocean, and also in Long Island Sound, Peconic Bay, and Great South Bay (Morreale et al. 1992, Shoop and Kenney 1992). Resident species are those that breed, nest, and hibernate locally and live on and around Fire Island year round. Because resident species are more affected by activities and conditions on Fire Island than migrant species, and thus more directly under the control of the National Park Service, they were the primary focus.

There have been no prior attempts to broadly sample Fire Island's amphibians and reptiles, and the "historic" data on species occurrence is very piecemeal (Overton 1914; Murphy 1950; Smith 1962, 1963; Yeaton 1974; Northup 1986; Meyer 1988; Barcia 1996; Caldecutt 1997; Klemens 1997; Williamson 1999; Putnam 1999). Of 38 species of amphibians and reptiles historically resident on Long Island (Noble 1927), a total of 11 resident species have previously been reported from Fire Island (Appendix A). These include three anurans (Fowler's toad, *Bufo fowleri;* southern leopard frog, *Rana sphenocephala*; and the American bullfrog, *Rana catesbiena,* a recent arrival), five turtles (snapping turtle, *Chelydra serpentina*; Eastern mud turtle, *Kinosternon s. subrubrum*; Eastern box turtle, *Terrapene c. carolina*; spotted turtle, *Clemmys guttata*; and Northern diamond-backed terrapin, *Malaclemys t. terrapin*), and three snakes (black racer, *Coluber constrictor*; eastern garter snake, *Thamnophis s. sirtalis*; and Eastern hog-nosed snake, *Heterodon platirhinos*). Of these, the mud turtle is listed as endangered by New York State, and the box turtle, spotted turtle, and hognose snake are of "special concern" (NYDEC 2000). In addition, McCormick (1975) states the painted turtle (*Chrysemys picta*) is known to occur on Fire Island, but Northup (1986) states it has not been documented. Although common and widespread on Long Island proper (Yeaton 1974), there are no records of painted turtles on FIIS in spite of it being a very conspicuous species. Therefore, we did not consider painted turtle as historically present on FIIS.

The inventory sought all of FIIS's likely resident herpetofauna, but the four state-listed species noted above were considered high priority "targets". Because the expected species are broad in terms of taxonomic groups and habitat affinity, the inventory employed a variety of methods in a number of habitats. Choice of sampling sites, timing, and amount of sampling effort focused the effort towards target species, but because methods were generalized, data on the more common species were also obtained. Six standardized survey methods were used in the inventory, which was conducted in 2002 and 2003. Incidental encounters were also recorded to provide additional information on species presence and distribution. The habitat type of all sites where amphibians and reptiles were found was described, and the species and the habitat types they occupied were analyzed.

Study Area

Fire Island extends 55 km (32 miles) from Democrat Point east to Moriches Inlet, forming a barrier beach between Great South Bay and the Atlantic Ocean. The island is divided into a number of federal, state, county, and private holdings that include Robert Moses State Park on the western end and Smith Point County Park on the eastern end (Figure 1). The area of FIIS, which includes all of the preceding except Robert Moses State Park, totals 7924 ha (19,580 acres), of which nearly 6070 ha (15,000 acres) are the open waters of Great South Bay and the Atlantic Ocean. The remainder of the park (1762 ha, 4354 acres) consists of primary dune, swale, secondary dune, shrub thicket, maritime forest, freshwater wetlands, and tidal marsh habitats typical of barrier islands, as well as 916 acres of heavily developed residential area within 17 private communities that pre-date the park's establishment. Of FIIS's total acreage, 6241 are Federal, 12,423 are non-Federal public, and 916 are private. In 1980, a 559 ha (1381 acres) federally-owned portion of the park, on the eastern part of the island, was designated by Congress as the Otis Pike Wilderness Area (OPWA). It is the only federally-designated wilderness area in New York State.

The pattern of land ownership between the west end of the island (Robert Moses State Park) and the east end (Smith Point County Park) is one where federal and private lands alternate. Consequently, the 17 private communities within the park, which are primarily on the western half of the island, effectively divide National Park Service holdings into patches or tracts of varying size. Going from west to east, the largest tracts of NPS property on the island are Lighthouse tract (155 acre), Sailor's Haven/Sunken Forest (168 acre), Talisman (79 acre), and Watch Hill-OPWA (1497 acres) (Figure 1). OPWA is 11 km (7 miles) of undeveloped barrier island habitat from Watch Hill east to Smith Point Visitor's Center. Access in this area is limited to foot traffic from September through March, and restricted vehicle traffic is allowed on the beach during the fall and winter months.

Herpetological habitats on FIIS include two permanent ponds (Kismet Pond, Sailor's Haven Maintenance Pond), numerous temporary ponds, marshes, and cranberry bogs (both open and closed canopy), tidal marshes along Great South Bay, beach grass/beach heather/low thicket, and holly/mixed forest (McCormick 1975).

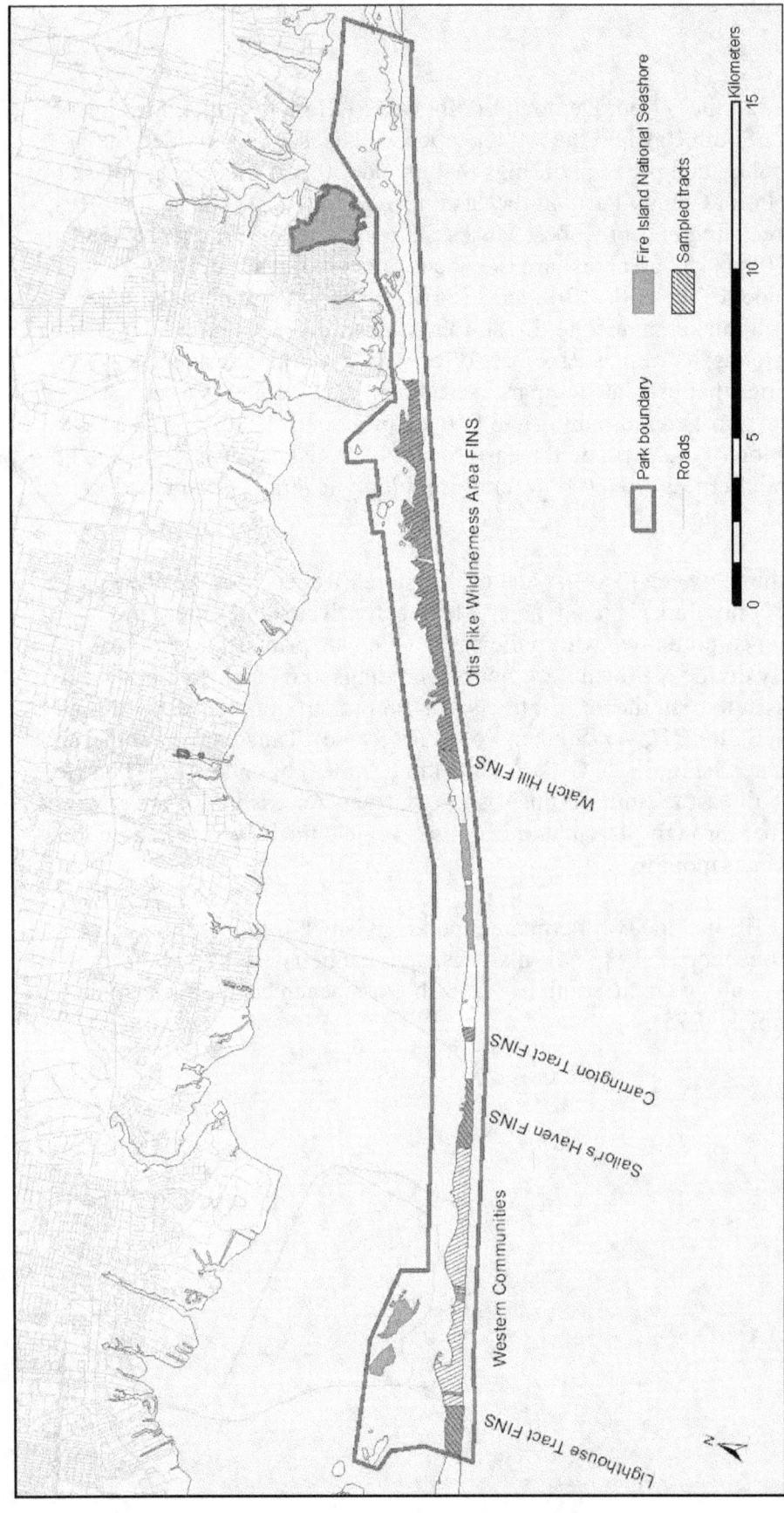

Figure 1. Overview map of Fire Island National Seashore showing patterns of land ownership and location of major NPS-owned tracts.

Methods

Sampling Overview

We sampled FIIS with a three person crew as part of an effort to survey the herpetofauna of three NPS units over the course of the 2002 field season. Because the herpetofauna of the northeast United States consists of a variety of species, each with differing periods of activity (which can also vary somewhat annually), we distributed sampling effort over the course of the spring and summer activity season. Given this, and the logistics of sampling three separate NPS units on Long Island (FIIS; William Floyd Estate NHS, Mastic; Sagamore Hill NHS, Oyster Bay) we sampled them in bouts that varied in duration in proportion to each's size and presumed faunal/zoogeographic complexity. Over the course of a month the crew sampled one and then moved on to the next, such that a full round of sampling was conducted each month during the months of April, May, June, August, and September. For FIIS, each monthly sampling bout was generally two weeks long.

The general approach of sampling was to balance the need for standardized methods and quantifiable results with the primary goal of determining species presence. Since amphibians and reptiles found at FIIS are variable in habitat use and seasonal patterns of detectability, we employed a number of methods, both general and habitat/taxa specific. These were; Anuran Calling Surveys (ACS), Coverboard Surveys (CB), Turtle Trap Surveys (TTS) and Minnow Trap Surveys (MTS), Habitat or Area-specific Visual-encounter Surveys (VES), Drift Fences (DF), and Incidental Encounters (IE). We employed general methods (i.e. VES) across all habitats for the entire field season, whereas habitat/taxa specific methods were employed at those times of the year when the target species/habitat are known to be most efficiently sampled.

Because an important goal of these inventories was to better document species of management concern ("target species"), we emphasized methods sensitive to these species. The combination of methods chosen recognized that multiple methods were often necessary to detect the wide range of potentially-occurring species and that some species are difficult to detect due to rarity or behavior. Thus, a degree of redundancy was needed to increase the likelihood of encountering these rare/hard to find species, most all of which were "target species". Collectively, the methods we employed were designed to provide a comprehensive list of species occurrence and a reasonable estimate of relative abundance and habitat use. We divided habitats into two categories, wetland or upland, and further sub-divided these into seven habitat types to provide a description of each survey site (Appendix B). Although not a natural habitat, "developed" was considered a habitat type to describe the location of incidental encounters within communities.

Site selection for standardized surveys was designed to sample across the range of habitat types present as well as to be spatially balanced. Given the linear nature of Fire Island, the fragmentation of NPS lands by private development, and the logistics of field work, we viewed the NPS-owned portions of FIIS as a series of patches or tracts, containing a variety of upland and wetland habitat types. We used maps and field reconnaissance to identify the ponds/wetlands, tidal saltmarsh/ditches, beach grass, low thicket, and woodland habitats present within each patch from Robert Moses State Park to the eastern limit of OPWA. Because there were more patches than could be sampled, we considered the general positive relationship between patch size and species richness, and used location on the island and patch size as the primary criteria for selecting patches to sample. Occurrence of rare or unique habitat types or historic presence of rare species was also considered. Within each of the following patches, we sampled both upland and wetland habitats: Lighthouse tract; Sailor's Haven-Sunken Forest; Carrington tract (wetland only); and Watch Hill-OPWA (Table 1; Figures 2, 3, 4, 5).

Marking, Measurement, and Aging/Sexing of Captured Animals

Captured animals were treated differently in terms of marking and measurements, with exact details determined by whether a species was a "target" species, as well as the inherent ability to mark a species. While several different methods were employed to capture/sample animals, details of marking and measuring were based on details of species, not method of capture.

We classified amphibians as larvae or adult-form, and adult-form individuals into age categories (metamorph, juvenile, adults) but did not mark, measure, or weigh them. We measured snakes' snout-vent length (SVL), total length (TL), and mass, and sexed them based on degree of tail contour (Conant and Collins 1998), but did not mark them. We marked all turtles for individual identification, with each given a unique set of notches in the marginal scutes, using a code system modified from Cagle (1939). For all turtles captured, we measured carapace length (CL), carapace width (CW), plastron length (PL), and mass. Turtles were sexed based on external features for each species described in Ernst et al. (1994). Individuals were classified as adult, as opposed to juvenile, based on the following size criteria: snapping turtles, males with CL >210 mm and females with CL>200 mm (Congdon et al. 1987, 1992, Ernst et al. 1994); spotted turtles, PL>80 mm Graham (1995); mud turtles CL>75mm (Frazer et al. 1991); box turtles CL>120 mm (Dodd 2001).

Anuran Calling Surveys

Anuran calling surveys (ACS) were conducted using the Wisconsin frog and toad survey method (Heyer et al. 1994). ACS records the presence of species calling at specific sites and provides an index of abundance based on the calling intensity. Call index (CI) values and criteria for assigning them are; 0 = no calls, 1 = individuals can be counted (no overlapping of calls), 2 = overlapping of calls (can still be counted), 3 = full chorus-calls are constant and individually indistinguishable. The surveyors arrived at each sample site at least one half-hour after dusk. Surveyors listened for anuran calls for five minutes, recording species heard, the number of individuals heard, if any, and the call index for each species.

We surveyed 13 pre-selected sites between March 26 and June 24, 2002. Although the original plan called for sampling each site an equal number of times, the exigencies of field work prevented this, and sites were sampled from two to seven times, as detailed below. Because of the unequal number of sampling occasions, and the low number of occasions at some sites, there is some bias against detecting species with low detection probabilities. Multiple call counts at a site, conducted over the entire spring and early summer months are necessary to document species presence over time, as different anuran species are active at different times of the season (Conant and Collins 1998; Crouch and Paton 2002).

Table 1. Overview of standardized survey sites and sampling methods used at each site on Fire Island National Seashore. ACS = Anuran Calling Survey; VES = Visual Encounter Survey; CB = Coverboard; TTS = Turtle Trap Survey; MTS = Minnow Trap Survey; DF = Drift Fence.

Tract	Sample Site	Habitat Type	ACS	VES	CB	TTS	MTS	DF
Lighthouse	Kismet Interior	beachgrass/beach heather/low thicket		X	X			
Lighthouse	Sedge Meadow east Kismet Pond	non-tidal marsh	X	X				
Lighthouse	Kismet Pond	permanent pond	X	X		X	X	X
Lighthouse	Kismet Bayside	tidal marsh/swamp		X				
Carrington	Carrington Swamp	non-tidal marsh	X	X				
Sailor's Haven	Sailor's Haven Interior	beachgrass/beach heather/low thicket		X	X			
Sailor's Haven	Sunken Forest	holly/mixed forest		X				
Sailor's Haven	Sailor's Haven Maintenance Pond	permanent pond	X	X		X	X	
Sailor's Haven	Sunken Forest Pond 2	temporary pond	X	X		X	X	
Sailor's Haven	Sunken Forest Pond 4	temporary pond	X	X		X	X	
Sailor's Haven	Sunken Forest Pond 6	temporary pond	X	X		X	X	
Sailor's Haven	Sunken Forest Pond 7	temporary pond	X	X		X	X	
Sailor's Haven	Sunken Forest Pond 8	temporary pond	X	X		X		
Sailor's Haven	Sailor's Haven Bayside	tidal marsh/swamp	X	X				
Watch Hill	Watch Hill Interior	beachgrass/beach heather/low thicket		X	X			
Watch Hill	Watch Hill Boardwalk Pond	temporary pond				X		
Watch Hill	Watch Hill Pond 37	temporary pond	X	X		X		
Watch Hill	Watch Hill Bayside	tidal marsh/swamp		X				
Watch Hill	Watch Hill Ditches	tidal marsh/swamp				X		
OPWA	Old Inlet to Bellport Beach (interior)	beachgrass/beach heather/low thicket		X	X			
OPWA	Smith Point to Old Inlet (interior)	beachgrass/beach heather/low thicket		X	X			
OPWA	Hospital Point Cranberry Bog	non-tidal marsh	X	X				
OPWA	Molasses Point Marsh	non-tidal marsh				X	X	
OPWA	Transect 4 Marsh	non-tidal marsh	X	X		X	X	
OPWA	Bigfoot Pond	temporary pond	X	X		X		

Table 1. Continued.

Tract	Sample Site	Habitat Type	ACS	VES	CB	TTS	MTS	DF
OPWA	Bellport Bay Ditches	tidal marsh/swamp				X		
OPWA	Hospital Point Ditches	tidal marsh/swamp				X		
OPWA	Molasses Point Ditches	tidal marsh/swamp		X		X		
OPWA	Old Inlet to Bellport Beach (bayside)	tidal marsh/swamp		X				
OPWA	Smith Point to Old Inlet (bayside)	tidal marsh/swamp		X				

8

Fire Island National Seashore
Herpetological Survey

Sampling methods and locations - Lighthouse Tract

July 2005
Data source: The National Park Service, the U.S. Geological
Survey, and the U.S. Department of Commerce U.S. Census
Bureau Geography Division.

Figure 2. Lighthouse tract sampling sites and visual encounter survey areas used in herpetofaunal inventory on Fire Island National Seashore, 2002 and 2003.

Fire Island National Seashore
Herpetological Survey

Sampling methods and locations - Sailor's Haven-Sunken Forest

July 2005
Data source: The National Park Service, the U.S. Geological
Survey, and the U.S. Department of Commerce U.S. Census
Bureau Geography Division.

Figure 3. Sunken Forest/Sailors Haven tract sampling sites and visual encounter survey areas used in herpetofaunal inventory on Fire Island National Seashore, 2002 and 2003.

Fire Island National Seashore
Herpetological Survey

Sampling methods and locations – Watch Hill

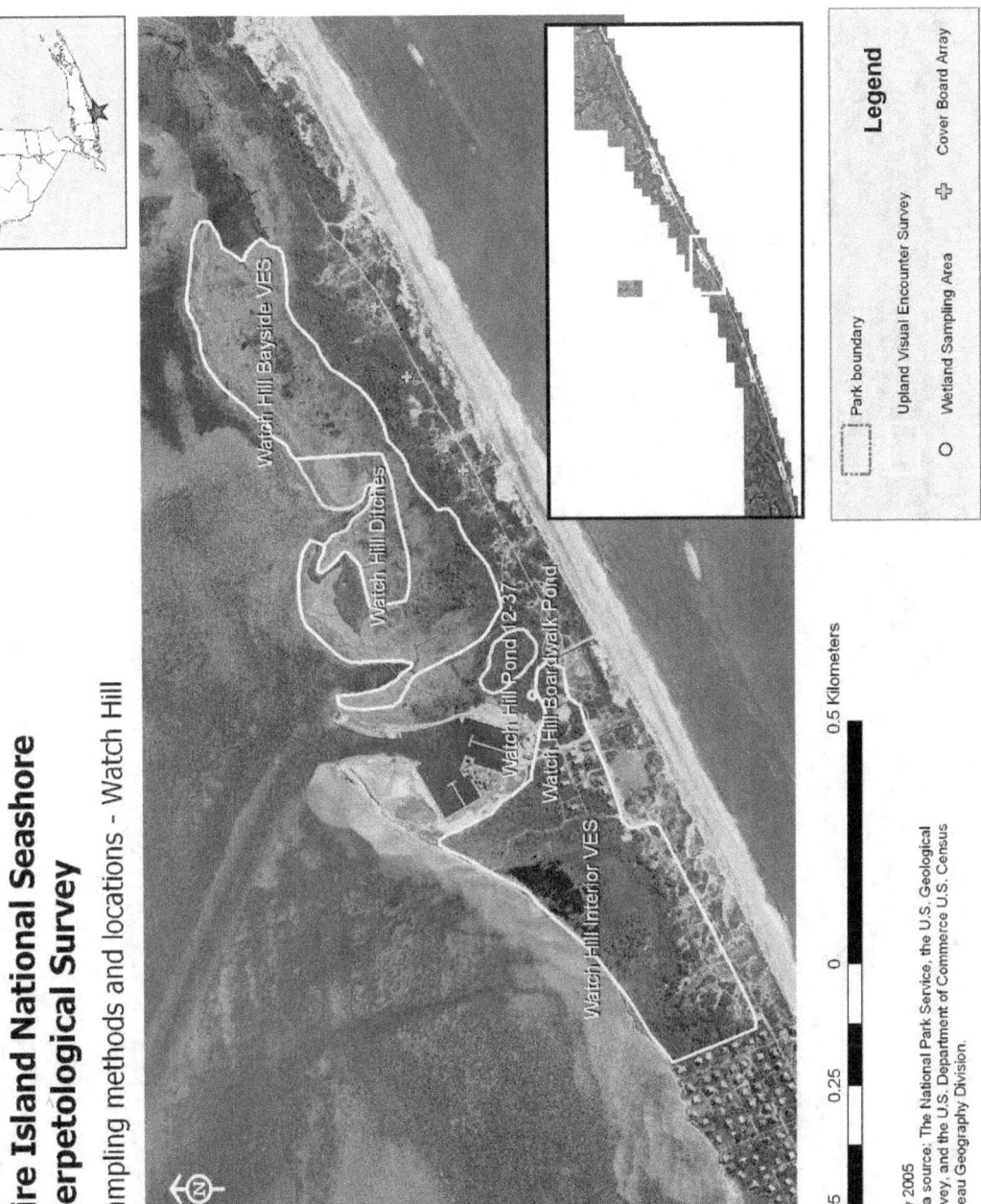

Figure 4. Watch Hill tract sampling sites and visual encounter survey areas used in herpetofaunal inventory on Fire Island National Seashore, 2002 and 2003.

Fire Island National Seashore
Herpetological Survey

Sampling methods and locations - Otis Pike Wilderness Area

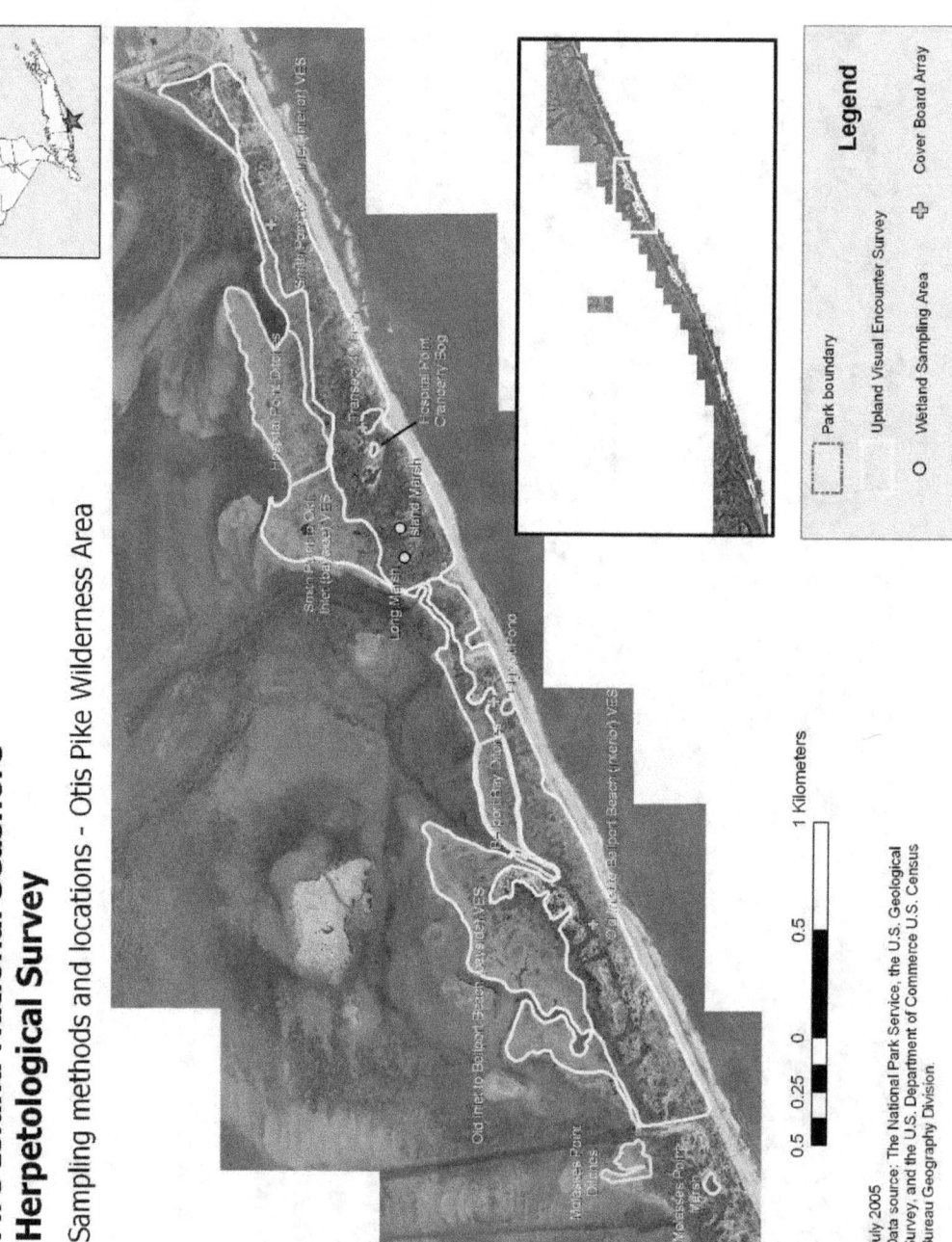

July 2005
Data source: The National Park Service, the U.S. Geological
Survey, and the U.S. Department of Commerce U.S. Census
Bureau Geography Division.

Legend

☐ Park boundary

Upland Visual Encounter Survey

○ Wetland Sampling Area

✚ Cover Board Array

Figure 5. Otis Pike Wilderness Area tract sampling sites and time-constrained search areas used in herpetofaunal inventory on Fire Island National Seashore, 2002 and 2003.

Survey sites and number of sample occasions were:
- Bigfoot Pond-3
- Carrington Swamp-2
- Hospital Pt. Cranberry Bog-3
- Kismet Pond-7
- Sedge Meadow E. Kismet Pond-2
- Sailor's Haven Maintenance Pond-4
- SF Pond #2-5 occasions
- SF Pond #4-5
- SF Pond #6-5
- SF Pond #7-5
- SF Pond #8-5
- Transect 4 Marsh-3
- Watch Hill Pond #37-4

Visual Encounter Surveys

We conducted habitat-specific visual encounter surveys (VES) (Crump and Scott 1994) in all habitats likely to support amphibians and reptiles, i.e. ponds/wetlands, bayside saltmarsh/ditches, beach grass, low thicket, and woodland. Each wetland or upland VES area was searched thoroughly and time taken to do so recorded. Searchers used an approach intended to maximize the numbers and diversity of captures by moving through the area and searching under the best available cover (e.g. logs, boards, metal debris) favored by amphibians and reptiles (Bury and Raphael 1983), and by dip netting ponds (Heyer et al. 1994). Although the original plans called for sites within each habitat type to be sampled the same number of times, this was not always the case. We standardized results of VES as a capture rate (CR) for each species, calculated by dividing the total number of individuals recorded by the total search effort (person hours) spent for each search. Person hours are the total amount of time spent searching, multiplied by the number of people participating in the search.

Upland VES

Six upland areas were surveyed four to six times between 2 April and 3 September 2002, as detailed below. Start and end times, number of searchers, and the species, number, and sex of animals found were recorded.

Beachgrass/Beach Heather/Low thicket
- Kismet Interior-5 surveys, 7.1 search hours.
- Old Inlet to Bellport Beach (Interior)-5 surveys, 19.2 search hours.
- Sailor's Haven Interior- 5 surveys, 5.5 search hours.
- Smith Point to Old Inlet (Interior)-6 surveys, 20.7 search hours.
- Watch Hill Interior- 4 surveys, 3.3 search hours.

Holly/Mixed Forest
- Sunken Forest- 6 surveys, 12.8 search hours.

Wetland VES

Nineteen wetland sites were surveyed two to six times between 1 April and 6 September 2002, as detailed below. For pond and marsh habitats, surveys were conducted by traversing the entire pond or marsh, sampling with a dip-net for amphibian larvae and adults, as well as turtles, and snakes. Surveys in ditches and salt marsh habitat on the bayside were conducted from start to end points, searching in the ditches for turtles and along the flotsam line and into the shrubs and emergent vegetation for turtles and snakes. Start and end times, number of searchers, and the identification, number, and sex of individuals found were recorded.

Tidal Marsh/Swamp
- Kismet Bayside - 5 surveys, 2.8 search hours.
- Molasses Point Ditches- 5 surveys, 6.0 search hours.
- Old Inlet to Bellport Beach (bayside) - 6 surveys, 22 search hours.
- Sailor's Haven Bayside- 5 surveys, 4.5 search hours.
- Smith Point to Old Inlet (bayside) - 5 surveys, 16.5 search hours.
- Watch Hill Bayside- 6 surveys, 6.6 search hours.

Non-tidal Marsh
- Carrington Swamp- 3 surveys, 0.4 search hours.
- Hospital Pt. Cranberry Bog- 4 surveys, 1.2 search hours.
- Sedge Meadow E. of Kismet Pond- 3 surveys, 0.8 search hours.
- Transect 4 Marsh- 3 surveys, 0.9 search hours.

Permanent Pond
- Kismet Pond- 5 surveys, 4.4 search hours.
- Sailor's Haven Maintenance Pond- 5 surveys, 2.6 search hours.

Temporary Pond
- Bigfoot Pond (OPWA) - 2 surveys, 0.9 search hours.
- SF Pond 2- 6 surveys, 0.8 search hours.
- SF Pond 4- 6 surveys, 1.9 search hours.
- SF Pond 6- 6 surveys, 1.6 search hours.
- SF Pond 7- 6 surveys, 2.5 search hours.
- SF Pond 8- 6 surveys, 0.5 search hours.
- Watch Hill Pond 37- 4 surveys, 0.7 search hours.

Coverboards

We used coverboards (Grant et al. 1992) primarily to inventory snakes, but coverboards near wetlands were also expected to detect terrestrial amphibians. Boards were 0.6 m x 1.2 m (2' x 4') and made of corrugated sheet metal or plywood. In March 2002, coverboards were deployed at 12 beachgrass sites located near the edge of woodland and shrub habitat when possible. We placed eight boards five meters apart in linear "arrays" consisting of alternating wood and metal boards. Due to the challenge of accessing coverboard sites in remote areas of the island, we checked some sites more often than others. We checked coverboards one or four times each in April, two or three times each in May, one to three times each in June (except Watch Hill-none),

one or two times in July (except OPWA-none), one to three times in August, and two times (OPWA) in September.

Coverboard arrays were:
- Kismet Area – 2 arrays, 13 visits, 104 boardchecks each.
- OPWA – 4 arrays, 12 visits, 87 to 96 boardchecks each.
- Sailor's Haven – 3 arrays, 8 or 9 visits, 64 or 72 boardchecks each.
- Watch Hill – 3 arrays, 9 visits, 72 boardchecks each.

We calculated a capture rates (CR) as the number of snake captures under boards divided by the total number of board checks for each site. Each time a board was checked constituted a "board check". Therefore, a site with eight boards visited six times equaled 48 board checks. The number of snake captures per 100 coverboard checks was calculated as:

$$CR = \frac{(\# \, of \, snake \, captures)}{(total \, \# \, of \, board \, checks)} \times 100$$

Turtle Trap Surveys
We used welded-wire crab traps measuring 30.5cm x 30.5cm x 60.1cm (12"x12"x 24"), with a mesh size of 1.3cm x 2.5cm (0.5" x 1") primarily to sample shallow areas for small aquatic/semi-aquatic turtles such as spotted turtle and eastern mud turtle. We used funnel traps made of D-shaped metal hoops and 2.6cm (1") nylon mesh to sample deeper wetlands areas for aquatic turtles such as painted and snapping turtles (Harless and Morlock 1989). One to six traps, baited with sardines in vegetable oil and checked daily, were set for three or five-day periods between 30 April and 7 June 2002 at 14 sites. To better understand the status of the eastern mud turtle on FIIS we conducted follow-up trapping daily in Bellport Bay Ditches, Bigfoot Pond, and Transect 4 Marsh, from 17 May to 5 June 2003. We quantified turtle abundance as a capture rate, captures per 100 trapnights.

Trap sites in 2002 were:

Tidal Marsh/Swamp

- Bellport Bay Ditches (2, 5-day trap periods, 5 traps)
- Hospital Pt. Ditches (2, 5-day trap periods, 5 traps)
- Molasses Pt. Ditches (2, 5-day trap periods, 2 traps)
- Watch Hill Ditches (2, 5-day trap periods, 4 traps)

Non-tidal Marsh

- Molasses Pt. Marsh (2, 5-day trap periods, 1 trap)

Permanent Pond

- Kismet Pond (2, 5-day trap periods, 3 to 4 traps)
- Sailor's Haven Maint. Pond (2, 5-day trap periods, 2 traps)

- Bigfoot Pond (2, 5-day trap periods, 2 traps)
- SF Pond 2 (2, 5-day trap periods, 2 traps)
- SF Pond 4 (2, 5-day trap periods, 3 traps)
- SF Pond 6 (2, 5-day trap periods, 3 traps)
- SF Pond 7 (2, 5-day trap periods, 3 traps)
- Watch Hill Boardwalk Pond (1, 3-day trap period, 2 traps)
- Watch Hill Pond 37 (2, 5-day trap periods, 4 to 6)

Trap sites in 2003 were:
- Bellport Bay Ditches (1, 18-day trap period, 8 to 16 traps)
- Bigfoot Pond (1, 20-day trap period, 4 to 10 traps)
- Transect 4 Marsh (1, 17-day trap period, 8 to 10 traps)

Minnow Trap Surveys

We used wire mesh minnow traps measuring 15.2 cm x 15.2 cm x 30.5 cm (6"x 6"x 12") to sample shallow pond areas for adult and larval salamanders, adult and larval anurans, and aquatic snakes (Heyer et al. 1994). Two to three traps each were deployed at eight sites for either two or four five-day periods between 2 April and 1 August 2002. Since this method primarily captures amphibians, which were not marked for individual recognition, abundance was quantified as total captures (rather than unique individuals) per 100 trap nights.

Trap sites were:

Non-tidal Marsh

- Hospital Pt. Cranberry Bog (2, 5-day trap periods, 2 traps)
- Transect 4 Marsh (2, 5-day trap periods, 2 traps)

Permanent Pond

- Kismet Pond (4, 5-day trap periods, 2 to 3 traps)
- Sailor's Haven Maintenance Pond (4, 5-day trap periods, 2 traps)

Temporary Pond

- SF Pond 2 (4, 5-day trap periods, 2 traps)
- SF Pond 4 (4, 5-day trap periods, 2 to 3 traps)
- SF Pond 6 (4, 5-day trap periods, 2 to 3 traps)
- SF Pond 7 (4, 5-day trap periods, 2 to 3 traps)

Drift Fences

We sampled for all species in and around Kismet Pond with four drift fence arrays (Figure 6). Each array was made of plastic silt fencing stapled to wooden stakes and pitfall traps and consisted of three wings extending out in different directions from a central point where a 5-gallon bucket was dug into the sand. Each wing had one #10 coffee can on either side at the midpoint and another 5-gallon bucket at the end of each wing, for a total of 10 pitfall traps per array (Heyer et al. 1994). The drift fence was monitored in 2002 from 27 March to 26 June, and 29 July to 22 August for a total of 116 nights and 4640 trap nights.

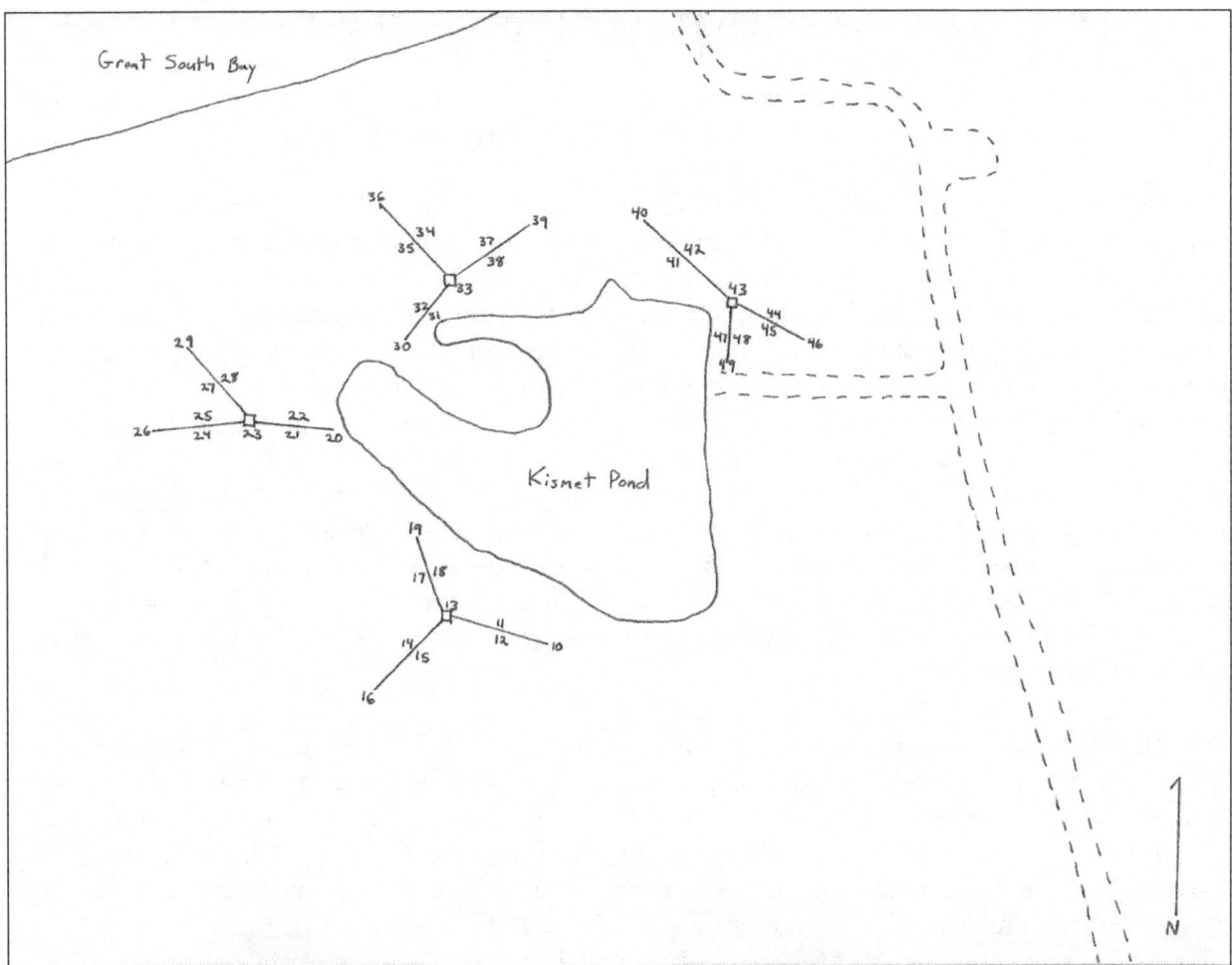

Figure 6. Kismet Pond drift fence and pitfall trap, Fire Island National Seashore, 2002.

Incidental Encounters
Any encounter with an amphibian or reptile not recorded as data in one of the standardized surveys was considered an incidental encounter (IE). We recorded these to augment data collected during formal surveys, including credible observations made by park staff and visitors. For each incidental encounter, species, life stage, method of documentation, as well as location, habitat, and UTM coordinates were recorded, though some of these data were sometimes missing from visitor reports. One particular incidental encounter, that of an eastern hog-nosed snake at Watch Hill on 5/14/07 (ML Lamont, pers. comm.), is significant as the only record of this species in the park since the 1970's (Putnam 1999). Because of its significance, this record has been incorporated into this report.

Quantifying Abundance and Distribution

Quantifying actual abundance of the species encountered was not possible for a number of reasons. The methods we used generally did not estimate actual population size, but rather provided a method-specific index of abundance, such as a capture rate (catch per unit effort). In addition, each of the seven methods provided a sample possibly biased towards a particular species or group of species or sex. Although sampling effort was divided among the different methods in an attempt to compensate for possible sampling bias, the amount of sampling bias, the extent to which the use of different methods may have balanced this bias, and the influence of other covariates, such as habitat type and breeding habits, were not estimated.

We derived an index of overall abundance for each species by summing the number of adult form individuals (as opposed to larvae) encountered during each of the seven survey methods. For visual encounter surveys, coverboard checks, turtle and minnow traps, and incidental encounters, the numbers of adult form individuals of a given species encountered during each sampling occasion were summed. Turtle shells (carapace/plastron), snake skins, and reptile nests were considered to represent one adult individual. Because we did not mark amphibians, for the purposes of estimating an overall index of abundance, we also treated reptiles as though they had not been marked. Because anuran calling surveys do not directly count adults, index values were converted to conservative estimates of the number of calling males present, based on data collected at Cape Cod National Seashore where both index values and estimates of numbers calling were made (Cook, unpublished data). Conservatively estimated numbers for Fowler's toad (*Bufo fowleri*) are Index 1=2 males calling and Index 2=6 males calling. Conservative estimates for calling Fowler's toads with no estimates from Cape Cod were Index 3=35 males calling (Crouch and Paton 2002).

Although the total numbers recorded for each species provide an index of overall abundance, it is an uncalibrated index, and its relationship to actual abundance is unknown. These numbers, and their derivatives, are best viewed as indicating the order of magnitude of a species' abundance and providing a reasonably accurate representation of relative and ranked abundance within each taxonomic group (i.e. frogs/toads, turtles, snakes). Although these numbers are of value for some inter-specific comparisons and community analysis, and are likely accurate in identifying abundant versus rare species, differences between species whose index of abundance are of the same order of magnitude may not reflect true differences in abundance.

Incidental encounters represent occasions when animals were encountered outside of formal standardized surveys. Such occasions include when a species that is not the target of a given survey method is encountered during a standard survey, such as when an amphibian is observed while checking a turtle trap. Thus incidental encounters may occur at sites where standardized surveys were conducted, but often occur at other locations in the park. A measure of a species' overall distribution was obtained by combining the number of standardized survey sites and incidental encounter locations at which it was recorded. This summed term is referred to as "localities". There were 41 localities. Of these, 30 were standardized survey sites and 11 were incidental encounter locations only.

Data Management

Common and scientific names and spellings are those of Crother et al. (2000, 2003). A Garmin III Plus Global Positioning System (GPS) unit was used to record the distance or area searched during time-constrained surveys and the coordinates of coverboard arrays (Appendix C). Coordinates of each site surveyed during standardized surveys and location identified during incidental encounters were also recorded. GPS locality data were recorded as Universal Transverse Mercator (UTM) (zone 18N) grid coordinates X=x-axis or Easting, and Y=y-axis or Northing, using NAD83.

Data collected in the course of this study, original data sheets, and voucher photos are archived with the National Park Service, Northeast Coastal and Barrier Inventory and Monitoring Network at the University of Rhode Island (http://science.nature.nps.gov/im/units/ncbn/).

Results

Overview of Park Herpetofauna

A total of 12 species, 10 resident and two migratory, were recorded during this survey or more recently. This includes an eastern hog-nosed snake observed in May 2007 in the Watch Hill area (ML Lamont, pers. comm.). Of the resident species, two were amphibian (both anurans), and eight were reptile (five turtles and three snakes). The two migratory species were sea turtles. By taxonomic group, anurans comprised 88 % of the 1170 individuals recorded, turtles 9 %, and snakes 3 %. The most frequently recorded species in each taxonomic group were Fowler's toad, snapping turtle and northern diamond-backed terrapin, and northern black racer (Table 2). No salamanders were recorded.

Animals were recorded at 37 of 41 sampling localities distributed throughout FIIS (Tables 3, 4; Figures 7-14). Based on frequency of occurrence, the most widespread species in each taxonomic group was Fowler's toad, eastern box turtle, and northern black racer. The most species rich sites were Kismet Interior and Sunken Forest with five species recorded. Five sites, Bellport Bay, Kismet Pond, Old Inlet to Bellport Beach (Bayside and Interior) and Watch Hill, each had four species (Table 4). By tract, the combined Watch Hill-OPWA tract had the greatest resident species richness, eight species, followed by the Lighthouse tract, with six species recorded. Similarly, these two tracts were first and second, respectively, in number of individuals recorded (Table 5).

By habitat, the greatest numbers of adults were recorded in permanent ponds (34% of individuals recorded), followed by beachgrass/beach heather/low thicket (21.6%), tidal marsh/swamp and marsh (14.4% each), non-tidal marsh (12.7%), temporary pond (9.1%), developed areas (5.9%), and holly/mixed forest (2.1%) (Table 2). Species richness was greatest in uplands, with 11 species recorded. However, this included two species of migratory marine turtles, washed up dead onto beaches in the developed communities. Of the 10 resident species recorded, nine were recorded in both uplands and wetlands. Eight species were recorded in both wetland and upland habitats, whereas American bullfrog and eastern hog-nosed snake were only recorded from wetland and upland respectively. For a single habitat type, species richness was greatest in beachgrass habitats and developed areas, each with seven species (Table 2).

Survey Method Summaries

Incidental encounters detected 10 of the 12 species recorded and, among the seven methods, produced the greatest total number of adults (46.8%), as well as the greatest numbers of Fowler's toad, northern black racer, eastern hog-nosed snake, and eastern garter snake (Tables 6 and 7). Of the standardized surveys, visual encounter surveys recorded the greatest number of species (7), 16.3% of all individuals recorded, and the greatest numbers of American bullfrog, eastern box turtle, and diamond-backed terrapin (Tables 6 and 7).Turtle trap surveys produced five species (5.7% of all individuals) and the greatest numbers of snapping turtle, spotted turtle, and mud turtle. The Kismet pond drift fence produced four species and the second greatest number of adults, 24.6%. The remaining methods, coverboards, minnow trap surveys, and anuran calling surveys produced relatively few species and total individuals (Tables 6 and 7).

Table 2. Number of adult form resident (r) and migrant (m) amphibian and reptile captures recorded during all surveys by habitat category on Fire Island National Seashore, in 2002 and 2003. Relative abundance (RA) within taxonomic groups is the total number of a species recorded divided by total number recorded within each group (order), expressed as a percentage. An eastern hog-nosed snake observed in May 2007 is included in this table.

	Wetland				Upland				RA (%)
	Tidal marsh/Swamp	Non-tidal marsh	Permanent pond	Temporary pond	Holly/mixed forest	Beachgrass/Beach heather/Low thicket	Developed	Total	(Rank)
Frogs									
Fowler's toad (r)	142	144	355	79	9	215	58	1002	97.1 (1)
American bullfrog (r)			30					30	2.9 (2)
Turtles									
Snapping turtle (r)	1	1	12	3	2	3	3	25	24.0 (1)
Eastern box turtle (r)	1			7	10	2	4	24	23.1 (2)
Northern diamond-backed terrapin (r)	19					6		25	24.0 (1)
Spotted turtle (r)				10	1			11	10.6 (5)
Eastern mud turtle (r)	4	4		8		1		17	16.3 (4)
Loggerhead sea turtle (m)							1	1	1.0 (6)
Leatherback sea turtle (m)							1	1	1.0 (6)
Snakes									
Northern black racer (r)	2				3	22	1	28	82.4 (1)
Eastern hog-nosed snake (r)							1	1	2.9 (3)
Eastern garter snake (r)			1			4		5	14.7 (2)
Total # of Adult Captures	169	149	398	107	25	253	69	1170	
% of Total Adult Captures	14.4%	12.7%	34.0%	9.1%	2.1%	21.6%	5.9%	100%	
Total # of Species	6	3	4	5	5	7	7	12	
		9				11			

22

Table 3. Distribution by habitat category of amphibians and reptiles recorded on Fire Island National Seashore, March to September 2002 and May to June 2003. Table entries indicate number of localities at which a species was recorded. Frequency of Occurrence (FO) is number of localities for a species divided by total number (41). Total number of localities includes both standardized survey sites (30) and incidental encounter locations (11). An eastern hog-nosed snake observed in May 2007 is included in this table.

	Wetland				Upland			Total	FO (%)
	Tidal marsh/Swamp	Non-tidal marsh	Permanent pond	Temporary pond	Holly/Mixed forest	Beachgrass/Beach heather/Low thicket	Developed		
Frogs									
Fowler's toad (r)	5	5	2	6	1	6	5	30	73.2%
American bullfrog (r)			1					1	2.4%
Turtles									
Snapping turtle (r)	1	1	2	3	1	1	1	10	22.4%
Eastern box turtle (r)	1			5	1	1	3	11	26.8%
Northern diamond-backed terrapin (r)	1	1		1		1		4	9.8%
Spotted turtle (r)				2	1			3	7.3%
Eastern mud turtle (r)	5					2		7	17.1%
Loggerhead sea turtle (m)							1	1	2.4%
Leatherback sea turtle (m)							1	1	2.4%
Snakes									
Northern black racer (r)	2				1	5	1	9	22.0%
Eastern hog-nosed snake (r)							1	1	2.4%
Eastern garter snake (r)			1			1		2	4.9%
# of Localities Sampled	10	6	2	9	1	6	7	41	

2

Table 4. Number of captures and total number of species recorded at each of 30 standardized surveys sites and 11 incidental encounter locations on Fire Island National Seashore. Frequency of Occurrence (FO) is number of localities at which a species was recorded divided by total number of localities (41). Species totals include all adult form individuals, plus nests (N) and shells (S). Includes an eastern hog-nosed snake observed in May 2007 at Watch Hill.

Localities (tract)	Fowler's toad	American bullfrog	Snapping turtle	Eastern box turtle	Eastern mud turtle	Spotted turtle	Northern diamond-backed terrapin	Loggerhead sea turtle	Leatherback sea turtle	Northern black racer	Eastern hog-nosed snake	Eastern garter snake	Total # of Adult Captures	% of Total	Total # of Species
Standardized Survey Sites															
Bellport Bay (OPWA)	91		1		4		1, 5S						102	8.7	4
Bigfoot Pond (OPWA)	54			1S	8								63	5.3	3
Carrington Swamp (Carrington)	10												10	0.9	1
Hospital Point Cranberry Bog (OPWA)	16												16	1.4	1
Hospital Point Ditches (OPWA)	6						1S						7	0.6	2
Kismet Bayside (Lighthouse)													0	0.0	0
Kismet Interior (Lighthouse)	12		3	2						2		4	23	2.0	5
Kismet Pond (Lighthouse)	310	30	9									1	350	29.9	4
Molasses Point Ditches (OPWA)							3N						3	0.3	1
Molasses Point Marsh (OPWA)	77												77	6.6	1
Old Inlet to Bellport Beach (bayside) (OPWA)	3			1S			1S			1			6	0.5	4
Old Inlet to Bellport Beach (interior) (OPWA)	10				1S		1, 2S			9, 3N			26	2.2	4
Sailor's Haven Bayside (Sailor's Haven)													0	0.0	0
Sailor's Haven Interior (Sailor's Haven)	2									3			5	0.4	2
Sailor's Haven Maint. Pond (Sailor's Haven)	45		3										48	4.1	2
Sedge Meadow east Kismet Pond (Lighthouse)													0	0.0	0
Smith Point to Old Inlet (bayside) (OPWA)							1, 4S, 3N					1	9	0.8	2

24

Localities (tract)	Fowler's toad	American bullfrog	Snapping turtle	Eastern box turtle	Eastern mud turtle	Spotted turtle	Northern diamond-backed terrapin	Loggerhead sea turtle	Leatherback sea turtle	Northern black racer	Eastern hog-nosed snake	Eastern garter snake	Total # of Adult Captures	% of Total	Total # of Species
Smith Point to Old Inlet (interior) (OPWA)	10									3, 1N			14	1.2	2
Sunken Forest (Sailor's Haven)	9		2	8,2S		1				3			25	2.1	5
Sunken Forest Pond 2 (Sailor's Haven)	1		1										2	0.2	2
Sunken Forest Pond 4 (Sailor's Haven)	4		1	1									6	0.5	3
Sunken Forest Pond 6 (Sailor's Haven)	12												12	1.0	1
Sunken Forest Pond 7 (Sailor's Haven)	2		1	3									6	0.5	3
Sunken Forest Pond 8 (Sailor's Haven)				1									1	0.1	1
Transect 4 Marsh (OPWA)	5		1		4								10	0.9	3
Watch Hill Bayside (Watch Hill)	2												2	0.2	1
Watch Hill Boardwalk Pond (Watch Hill)						2							2	0.2	1
Watch Hill Ditches (Watch Hill)													0	0.0	0
Watch Hill Interior (Watch Hill)	38						3N			1N			42	3.6	3
Watch Hill Pond 37 (Watch Hill)	6					8							14	1.2	2
Incidental Encounter Locations															
Lonelyville (western communities)	1												1	0.1	1
Ocean Bay Park (western communities)				1									1	0.1	1
Ocean Beach (western communities)								1					1	0.1	1
Old Inlet Marsh (OPWA)	40												40	3.4	1
OPWA (OPWA)	143												143	12.2	1
Point O'Woods (western communities)	8			1					1				10	0.9	3

Localities (tract)	Fowler's toad	American bullfrog	Snapping turtle	Eastern box turtle	Eastern mud turtle	Spotted turtle	Northern diamond-backed terrapin	Loggerhead sea turtle	Leatherback sea turtle	Northern black racer	Eastern hog-nosed snake	Eastern garter snake	Total # of Adult Captures	% of Total	Total # of Species
Sailor's Haven (Sailor's Haven)	2			2S									4	0.3	1
Saltaire (western communities)	1												1	0.1	1
Sunken Forest Carex Marsh (Sailor's Haven)	36												36	3.1	1
Sunken Forest Pond 5 (Sailor's Haven)				1									1	0.1	1
Watch Hill (Watch Hill)	46		3							1		1	51	4.4	4
Total # of Adult Captures (includes N and S)	1002	30	25	24	17	11	25	1	1	28	1	5	1170	100	12
Total # of Localities (includes N and S)	30	1	10	11	4	3	7	1	1	9	1	2			
FO (%)	73%	2%	24%	27%	10%	7%	17%	2%	2%	22%	2%	5%			

Fire Island National Seashore
Herpetological Survey

Frog and Snake Species Locations - Lighthouse Tract

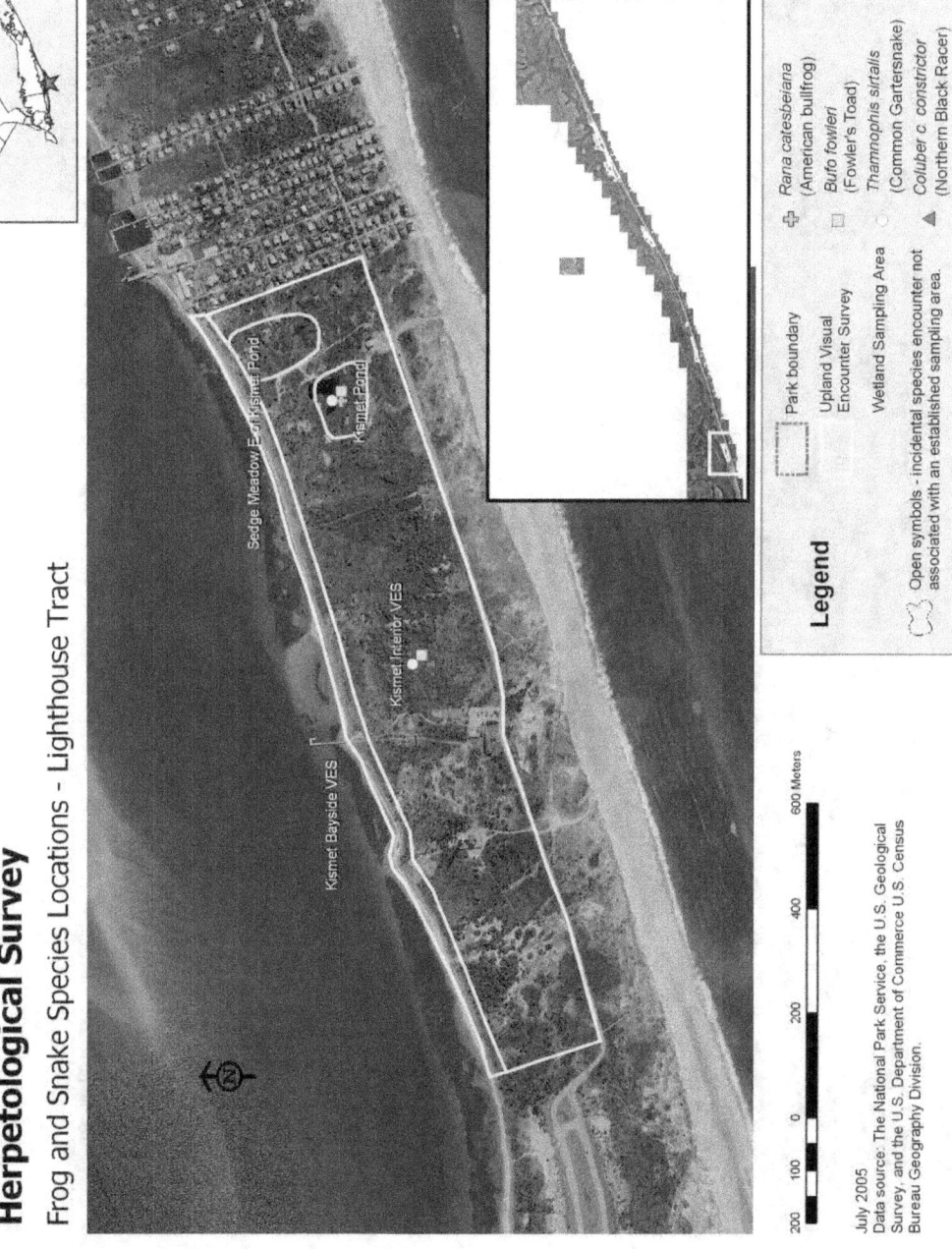

Figure 7. Location of frog and snake detections within the Lighthouse Tract, Fire Island National Seashore.

Figure 8. Location of turtle detections within the Lighthouse Tract, Fire Island National Seashore.

Fire Island National Seashore
Herpetological Survey

Frog and Snake Species Locations - Sailor's Haven-Sunken Forest

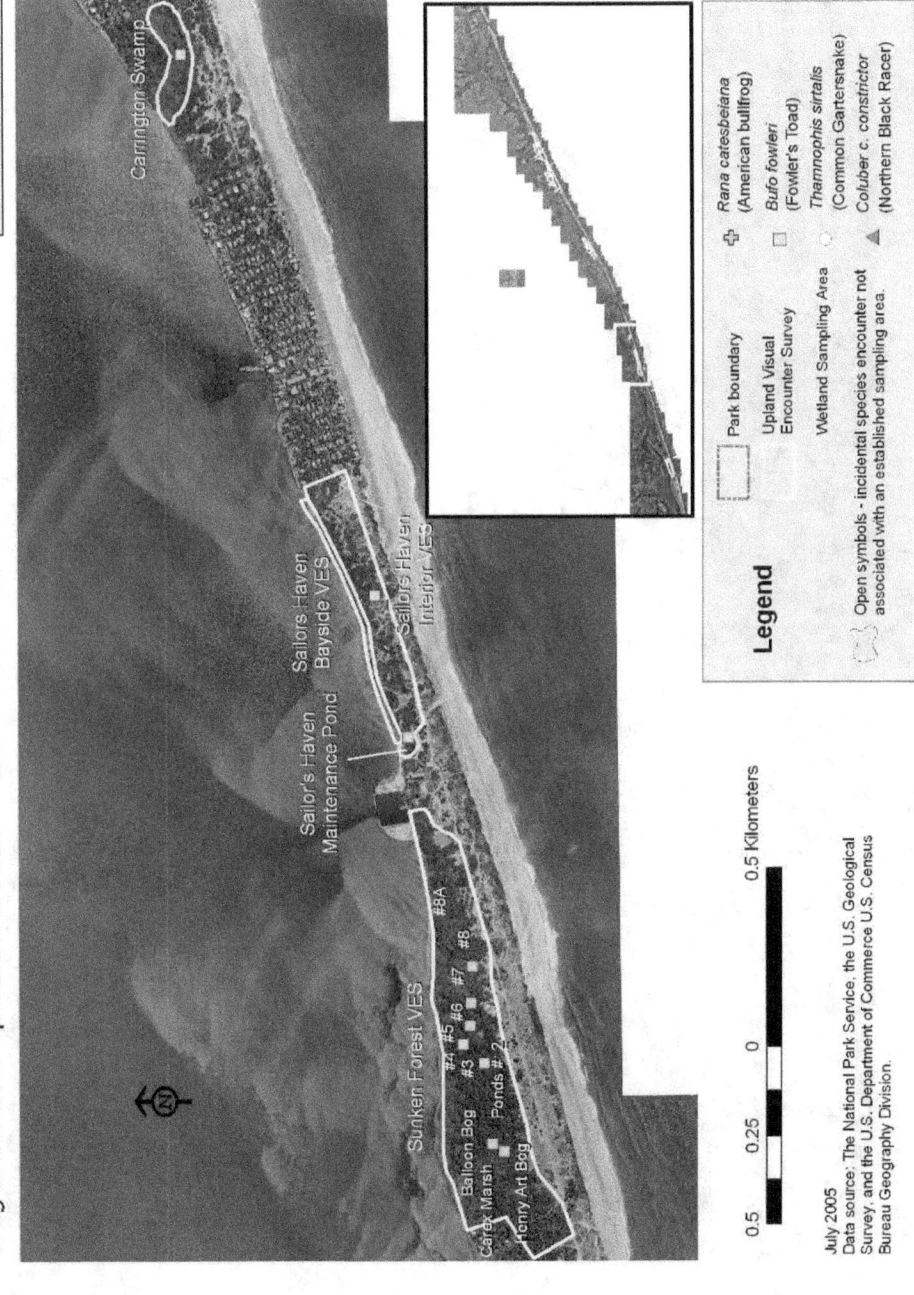

Figure 9. Location of frog and snake detections within Sailor's Haven/Sunken Forest Tract, Fire Island National Seashore.

Fire Island National Seashore
Herpetological Survey

Turtle Species Locations - Sailor's Haven-Sunken Forest

Carrington Swamp

Sailor's Haven
Bayside VES

Sailors Haven
Interior VES

Sailor's Haven
Maintenance Pond

Sailor's Haven
Maintenance Pond

Sunken Forest VES

#8A

#8

#7

#6

#5

#4

#3

Balloon Bog

Carex Marsh

Ponds #2

Henry Art Bog

Legend

⬚	Park boundary	
⬚	Upland Visual Encounter Survey	
☆	Wetland Sampling Area	

Open symbols - incidental species encounter not associated with an established sampling area.

⊕ *Chelydra serpentina* (Snapping Turtle)

□ *Terrapene carolina* (Box Turtle)

☆ *Kinosternon subrubrum* (Mud Turtle)

⊕ *Clemmys guttata* (Spotted Turtle)

○ *Malaclemys terrapin* (Diamond-back Terrapin)

▲ *Caretta caretta* (Loggerhead Sea Turtle)

◇ *Dermochelys coriacea* (Leatherback Sea Turtle)

0.25 0.125 0   0.25   0.5 Kilometers

July 2005
Data source: The National Park Service, the U.S. Geological Survey, and the U.S. Department of Commerce U.S. Census Bureau Geography Division.

Figure 10. Location of turtle detections within Sailor's Haven/Sunken Forest Tract, Fire Island National Seashore.

Fire Island National Seashore
Herpetological Survey

Frog and Snake Species Locations - Watch Hill

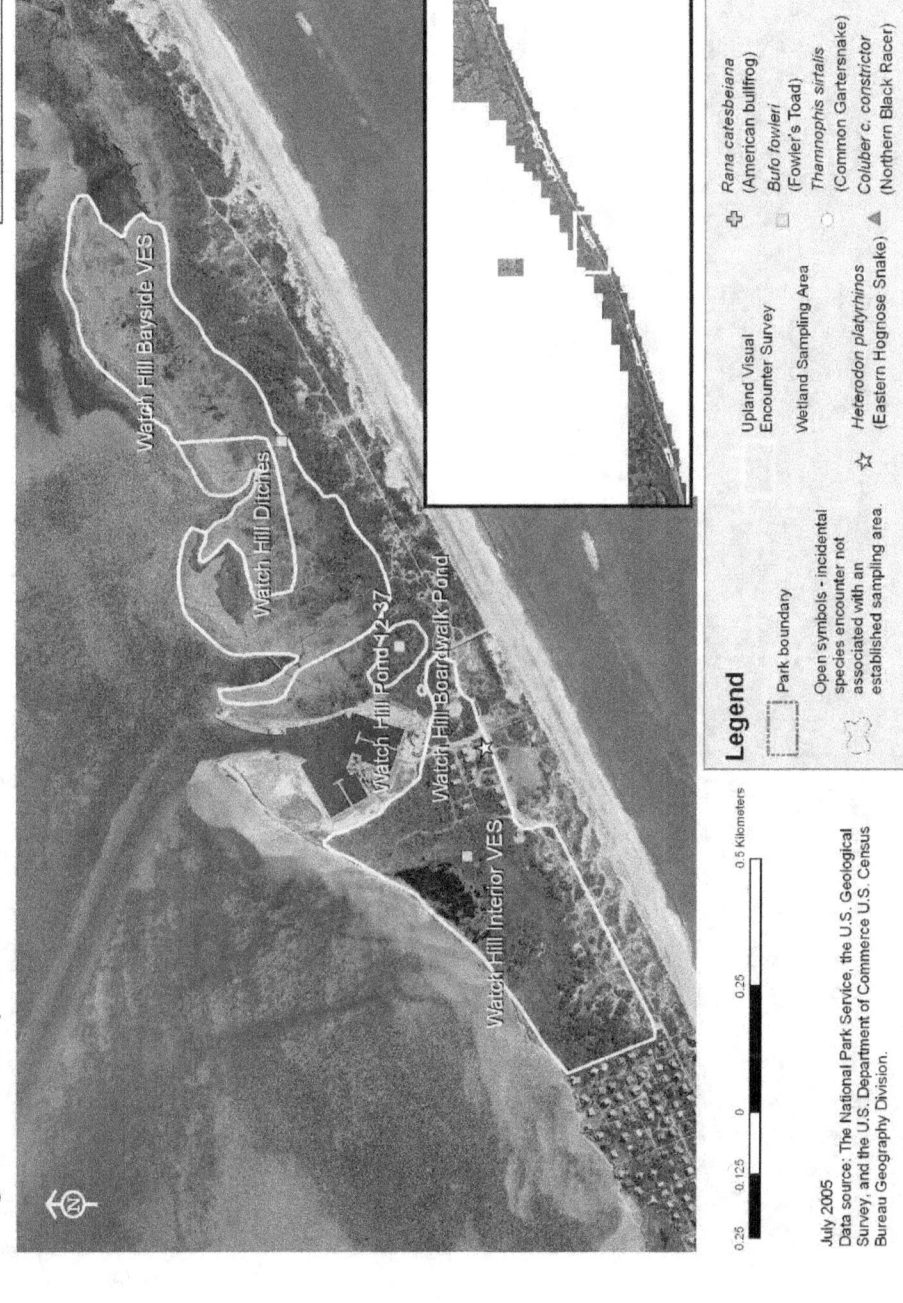

Figure 11. Location of frog and snake detections within Watch Hill Tract, Fire Island National Seashore.

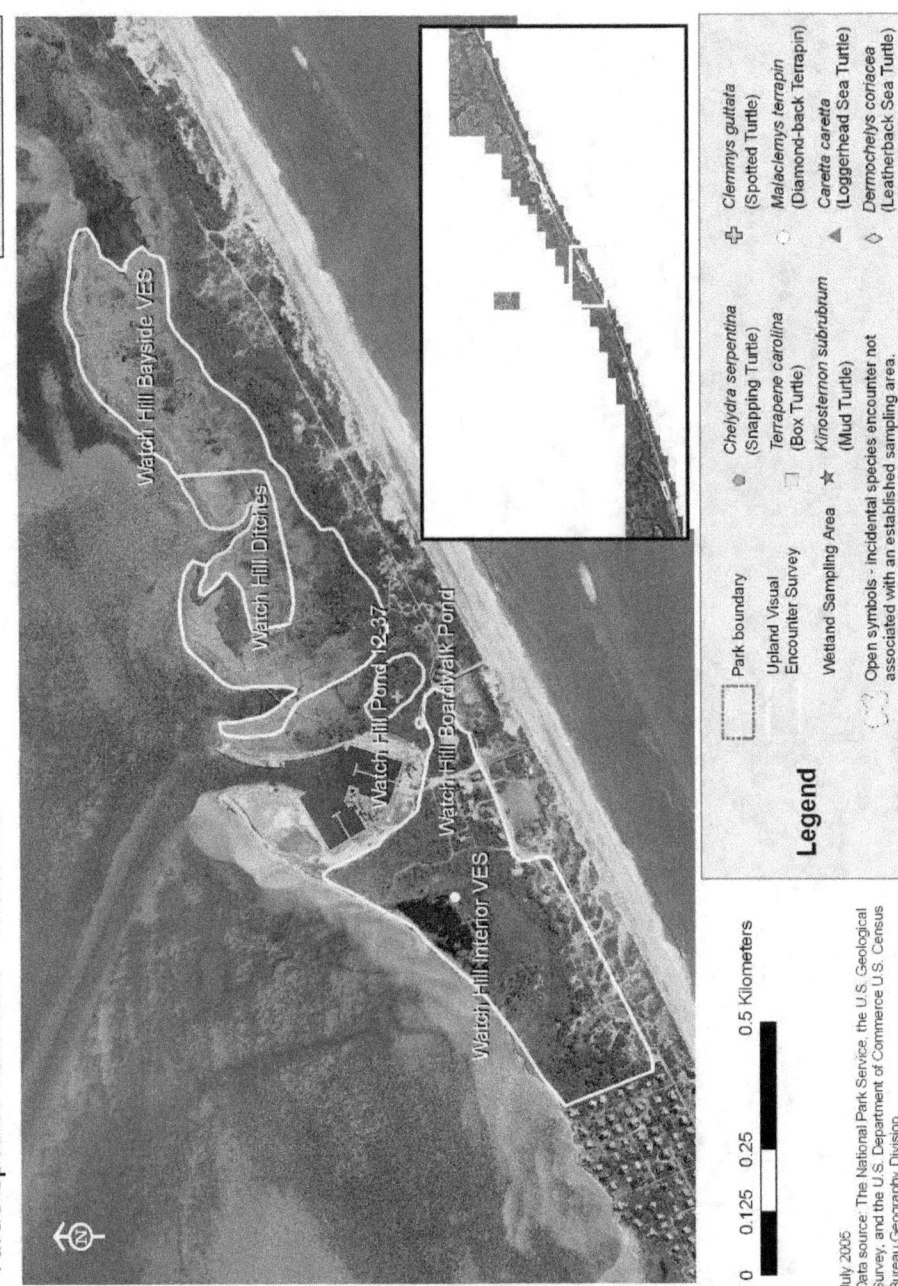

Figure 12. Location of turtle detections within Watch Hill Tract, Fire Island National Seashore.

Fire Island National Seashore
Herpetological Survey

Frog and Snake Species Locations - Otis Pike Wilderness Area

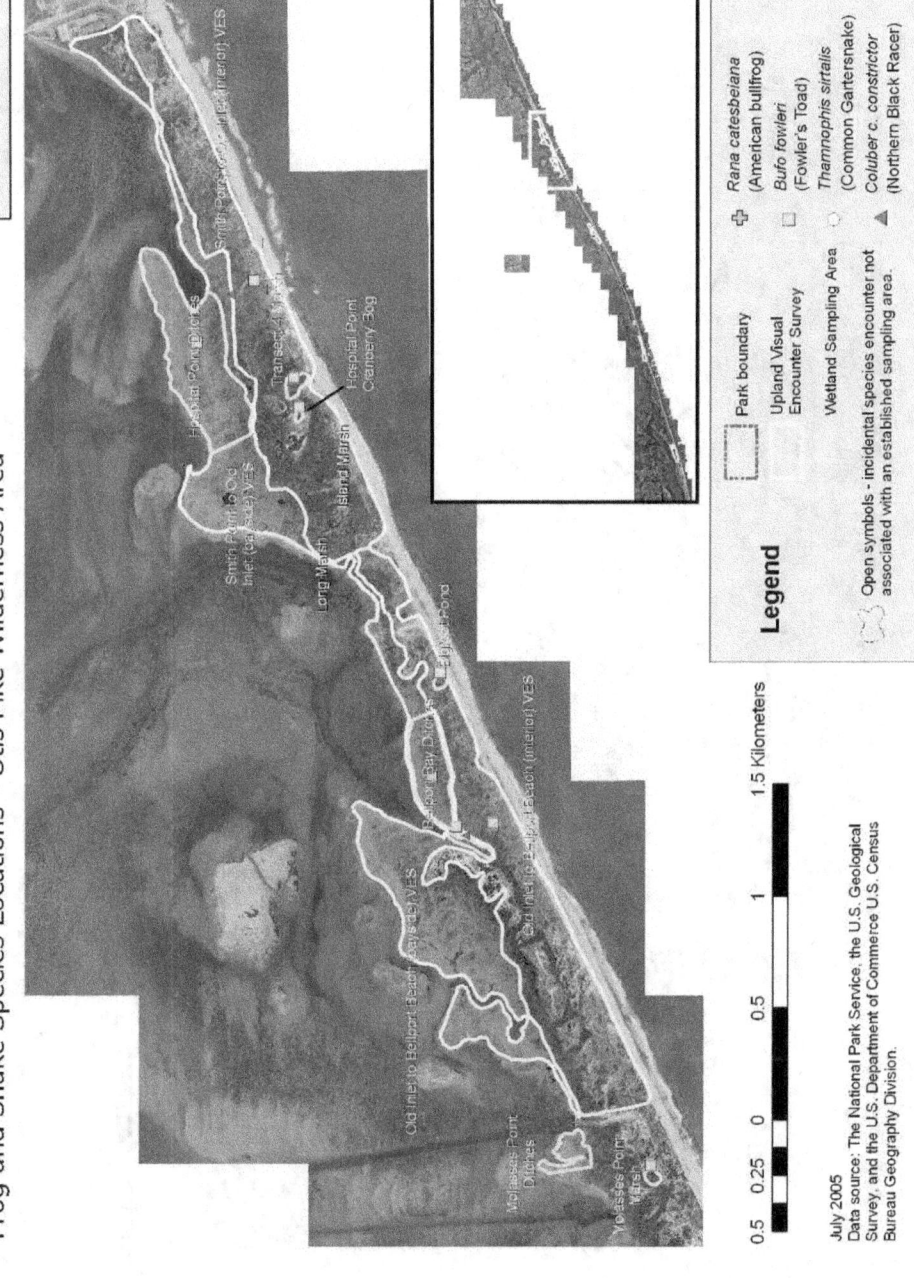

Figure 13. Location of frog and snake detections within Otis Pike Wilderness Area, Fire Island National Seashore.

Fire Island National Seashore
Herpetological Survey

Turtle Species Locations - Otis Pike Wilderness Area

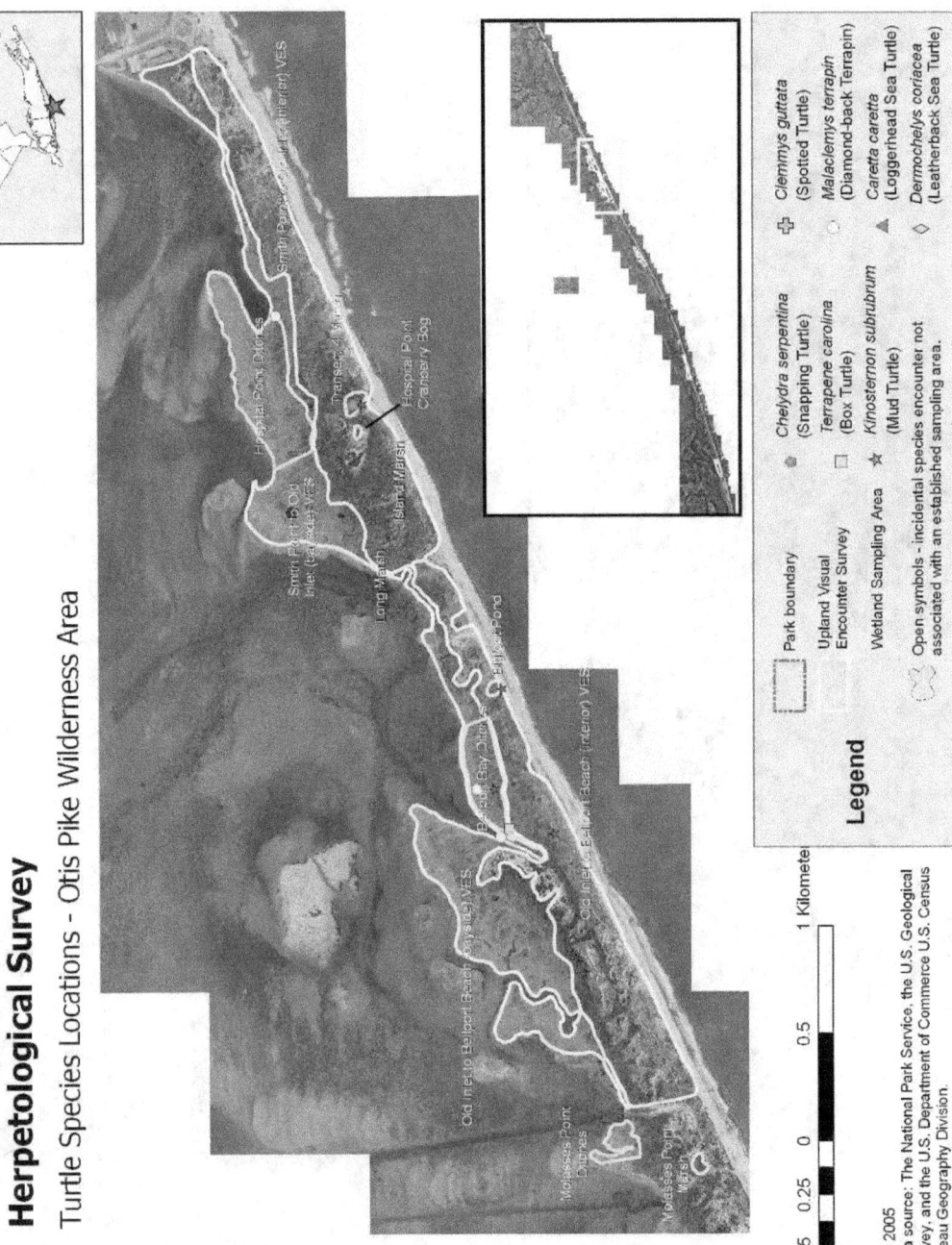

Legend

Park boundary

Upland Visual Encounter Survey

Wetland Sampling Area

Open symbols - incidental species encounter not associated with an established sampling area.

Chelydra serpentina (Snapping Turtle)

Terrapene carolina (Box Turtle)

Kinosternon subrubrum (Mud Turtle)

Clemmys guttata (Spotted Turtle)

Malaclemys terrapin (Diamond-back Terrapin)

Caretta caretta (Loggerhead Sea Turtle)

Dermochelys coriacea (Leatherback Sea Turtle)

0.5   0.25   0   0.5   1 Kilometer

July 2005
Data source: The National Park Service, the U.S. Geological Survey, and the U.S. Department of Commerce U.S. Census Bureau Geography Division.

Figure 14. Location of turtle detections within Otis Pike Wilderness Area, Fire Island National Seashore.

Table 5. Numbers of adult form amphibian and reptile captures recorded, and distribution of resident species by tract on Fire Island National Seashore. Western communities tract is section between Lighthouse tract and Sailor's Haven/Sunken Forest. Watch Hill and OPWA are shown separately, but collectively form a single tract. This table includes an eastern hog-nosed snake observed in May 2007.

Species	Lighthouse	Western Communities	Carrington	Sailor's Haven	Watch Hill	OWPA	Total Adults	# Tracts Present
Fowler's toad	322	10	10	113	92	455	1002	6
American bullfrog	30						30	1
Snapping turtle	12			8	3	2	25	4
Eastern box turtle	2	2		18		2	24	4
Eastern mud turtle						17	17	1
Spotted turtle				1	10		11	2
Northern diamond-backed terrapin					3	22	25	3
Northern black racer	2			6	2	18	28	4
Eastern hog-nosed snake					1		1	1
Eastern garter snake	5						5	1
Total # Adult Captures	373	12	10	146	111	516	1168	
% of total	31.9%	1.0%	0.9%	12.5%	9.5%	44.2%	100.0%	
Total # of Species	6	2	1	5	6	6	10	

35

Table 6. Number of amphibian and reptile captures recorded by each survey method on Fire Island National Seashore, March to September 2002 and May to June 2003. adl=adult form, including shells and nests, lrv=larvae. An eastern hog-nosed snake observed in May 2007 is included in this table.

Survey Method	Fowler's toad adl	Fowler's toad lrv	American bullfrog adl	American bullfrog lrv	Snapping turtle adl	Eastern box turtle adl	Eastern mud turtle adl	Spotted turtle adl	Northern diamond-backed terrapin adl	Loggerhead sea turtle adl	Leatherback sea turtle adl	Northern black racer adl	Eastern hog-nosed snake adl	Eastern garter snake adl	Total # of Species
Anuran Calling Survey	69														1
Visual Encounter Survey	129	71	20	4	3	12	1		16			10			7
Coverboard	3											3			2
Minnow Trap	1	161		1											2
Turtle Trap	32				10		16	8	1						5
Drift Fence	273		10		4									1	4
Incidental Encounter	495				8	12		3	8	1	1	15	1	4	10
Total Captures Recorded	1002	232	30	5	25	24	17	11	25	1	1	28	1	5	12

Table 7. Percentage of adult forms of each species recorded by each survey method. Derived from Table 6. An eastern hognose snake observed in May 2007 is included in this table.

Survey Method	Fowler's toad	American bullfrog	Snapping turtle	Eastern box turtle	Eastern mud turtle	Spotted turtle	Northern diamond-backed terrapin	Loggerhead sea turtle	Leatherback sea turtle	Northern black racer	Eastern hog-nosed Snake	Eastern garter snake	Total # Adults	% Total Adults
Anuran Call-Count	6.9												69	5.9
Visual Encounter Survey	12.9	66.7	12	50	5.9		64			35.7			191	16.3
Coverboard	0.3									10.7			6	0.5
Minnow Trap	0.1												1	0.1
Turtle Trap	3.2		40		94.1	72.7	4						67	5.7
Drift Fence	27.2	33.3	16									20	288	24.6
Incidental Encounter	49.4		32	40		27.3	32	100	100	53.6	100.0	80	548	46.8
% Total Captures	100	100	100	100	100	100	100	100	100	100	100	100		100
Total # of Captures	1002	30	25	24	17	11	25	1	1	18	1	5	1170	

37

Anuran Calling Surveys

Fowler's toad was the only anuran heard during calling surveys. It was recorded at five of 13 (38%) sites and on 7 of 55 (13%) sampling occasions (Table 8). A calling index of 3 was recorded only once during calling surveys, at Sailor's Haven maintenance pond. In contrast, a calling index of three was recorded incidentally on 10 occasions, at 10 different sites, mostly in OPWA.

Table 8. Maximum calling index (CI) and total numbers of calling males recorded during anuran calling surveys on Fire Island National Seashore, 2002.

Site	First Date	Last Date	# of Surveys	Fowler's toad # of Detections	Max CI	# males
Bigfoot Pond	10-Apr	4-Jun	3	0		
Carrington Swamp	2-May	28-May	2	2	2	10
Hospital Point Cranberry Bog	9-Apr	4-Jun	3	1	1	4
Kismet Pond	26-Mar	7-Jun	7	2	2	14
Sedge Meadow E. Kismet Pond	2-May	30-May	2	0		
Sailor's Haven Maint. Pond	1-Apr	28-May	4	1	3	35
Sunken Forest Pond 2	1-Apr	24-Jun	5	0		
Sunken Forest Pond 4	1-Apr	24-Jun	5	0		
Sunken Forest Pond 6	1-Apr	24-Jun	5	0		
Sunken Forest Pond 7	1-Apr	24-Jun	5	0		
Sunken Forest Pond 8	1-Apr	24-Jun	5	0		
Transect 4 Marsh	9-Apr	4-Jun	5	0		
Watch Hill Pond 37	1-Apr	27-May	4	1	2	6
Total	1-Apr	24-Jun	55	7	3	69

Visual Encounter Surveys

VES in uplands detected five species in six survey areas. Four species were recorded in beachgrass/beach heather/low thicket. Of these, Fowler's toad was the most abundant and widespread species, with 56 individuals recorded in all five areas surveyed, followed by northern black racer, eastern mud turtle, and northern diamond-backed terrapin (Table 9). Two species were detected during VES in the Sunken Forest, Fowler's toad (3 adults) and eastern box turtle (6 live adults and two carapaces) (Table 9).

VES at 19 wetland sites detected six species. Four of these were recorded in tidal marsh/swamp habitat, three in permanent and temporary ponds, and one in non-tidal marsh (Table 10). Fowler's toad was the most widespread species, recorded from 10 of 19 (53%) survey sites. It was also the most abundant species overall (70 individuals) and in three of four wetland types. American bullfrog was only recorded in Kismet Pond, but was overall the second most abundant species (20 adults) recorded in wetland VES. Northern diamond-backed terrapin and northern

Table 9. Number of amphibians and reptiles recorded during upland visual encounter surveys on Fire Island National Seashore, 2002. The number in parentheses is capture rate, i.e. (number of individuals divided by total search hours) x 100.

Habitat	Site	First Date	Last Date	# of Surveys	Search Hours	Fowler's toad adult	Fowler's toad voc	Northern black racer adult	Northern black racer nest	Eastern mud turtle shell	Eastern mud turtle shell	Northern diamond-backed terrapin nest	Eastern box turtle adult	Eastern box turtle shell	Total Adults	# of Species
Beachgrass-heather/ Low thicket	Kismet Interior	4-Apr	26-Aug	5	7.1	1 (14.1)									1 (14.1)	1
	Old Inlet to Bellport Beach Interior	10-Apr	3-Sep	5	19.2	8 (41.7)		2 (10.4)	1 (5.2)	1 (5.2)	1 (5.2)				10 (52.1)	3
	Sailor's Haven Interior	3-Apr	27-Aug	5	5.5	1 (18.2)		1 (18.2)							2 (36.4)	2
	Smith Point to Old Inlet Interior	9-Apr	3-Sep	6	20.7	9 (43.5)		2 (9.7)	1 (4.8)						11 (53.1)	2
	Watch Hill Interior	3-Apr	29-Aug	4	3.3	2 (60.6)	35 (1061)		1 (30.3)			3 (90.9)			37 (1121.2)	3
	Total			25	55.8	21 (37.6)	35 (62.7)	5 (9.0)	3 (5.4)	1 (1.8)	1 (1.8)	3 (5.4)			61 (66.3)	4
Holly forest	Sunken Forest	2-Apr	27-Aug	6	12.8	3 (23.4)							6 (46.9)	2 (15.6)	9 (70.3)	2
	Total			6	12.8	3 (23.4)							6 (46.9)	2 (15.6)	9 (70.3)	2

Table 10. Number of amphibians and reptiles recorded during wetland visual encounter surveys on Fire Island National Seashore, 2002. The number in parentheses is capture rate, i.e. (number of individuals divided by total search hours) x 100. Adl=adult, Lrv=larvae.

Habitat	Site	First Date	Last Date	# of Surveys	# Search Hours	Fowler's toad adl	Fowler's toad lrv	American bullfrog lrv	American bullfrog adl	Snapping turtle adl	N. diamond-backed terrapin adl	N. diamond-backed terrapin shell	N. diamond-backed terrapin nest	Eastern box turtle adl	Eastern box turtle shell	Northern black racer adl	# of Species
Tidal marsh-swamp	Kismet Bayside	3-Apr	26-Aug	5	2.8												0
	Molasses Point Ditches	10-Apr	3-Sep	5	6								3 (50)				1
	Old Inlet to Bellport Beach OPWA (bayside)	9-Apr	3-Sep	6	22	3 (14)					4 (18)				1 (4.5)	1 (4.5)	4
	Sailor's Haven Bayside	3-Apr	27-Aug	5	4.5												0
	Smith Point to Old Inlet OPWA (bayside)	11-Apr	3-Sep	5	16.5						2 (12)		3 (18)			1 (6.1)	2
	Watch Hill Bayside	2-Apr	29-Aug	6	6.6	2 (30)											1
	Total			32	58.4	5 (9)					6 (10)		6 (10)		1 (1.7)	2 (3.4)	4
Non-tidal marsh	Carrington Swamp	4-Apr	28-May	3	0.4												0
	Hospital Pt. Cranberry Bog	11-Apr	6-Sep	4	1.2	11 (917)	70 (5833)										1
	Sedge Meadow E. Kismet Pond	2-May	26-Aug	3	0.8												0
	Transect 4 Marsh	6-May	6-Sep	3	0.9												0
	Total			13	3.3	11 (333)	70 (2121)										1

Habitat	Site	First Date	Last Date	# of Surveys	# Search Hours	Fowler's toad		American bullfrog		Snapping turtle	Northern diamond-backed terrapin			Eastern box turtle		Northern black racer	# of Species
						adl	lrv	adl	lrv	adl	adl	shell	nest	adl	shell	adl	
Permanent pond	Kismet Pond	4-Apr	29-Aug	5	4.4	23 (523)	1 (23)	20 (455)	4 (90)								2
	Sailor's Haven Maintenance Pond	1-Apr	27-Aug	5	2.6	10 (385)				3 (115)							2
	Total			10	7.0	33 (471)	1 (14)	20 (286)	4 (57)	3 (43)							3
Temporary pond	Bigfoot Pond	4-Jun	6-Sep	2	0.9	2 (222)											1
	Sunken Forest Pond 2	1-Apr	27-Aug	6	0.8	1 (125)											1
	Sunken Forest Pond 4	1-Apr	27-Aug	6	1.9	4 (211)								1 (53)			2
	Sunken Forest Pond 6	1-Apr	27-Aug	6	1.6	12 (750)											1
	Sunken Forest Pond 7	1-Apr	27-Aug	6	2.5	2 (80)								2 (80)			2
	Sunken Forest Pond 8	1-Apr	27-Aug	6	0.5												0
	Watch Hill Pond 37	1-Apr	29-Aug	4	0.7												0
	Total			37	9.0	21 (233)								3 (33)			3

#Recorded

41

black racer were recorded at three and two tidal marsh sites, respectively. The majority of eastern box turtles recorded during wetland VES were in temporary ponds in the Sunken Forest (3 adults), and three snapping turtles was recorded from a permanent pond (Table 10).

Coverboards
Three northern black racers and three Fowler's toads were recorded by coverboards (Table 11). The snakes were at OPWA and Sailor's Haven and the toads were near Kismet Pond, Sailor's Haven, and Watch Hill. The capture rates for both species (0.3/100 board checks) were low.

Turtle Trap Surveys
Turtle trapping at 14 sites in 2002 produced a total of 18 captures of four species at seven sites (Table 12). Eight snapping turtles were each captured once at four sites. Snapping turtle was the only species trapped in both permanent and temporary pond habitats and was the most abundant turtle species in permanent pond habitat (CR=11.1/100 trap nights). There were a total of eight spotted turtle captures, all at Watch Hill Pond 37, involving five unique individuals, three of which were captured twice. The spotted turtle was the most abundant turtle in temporary pond habitat (CR=5.4). One eastern mud turtle and one northern diamond-backed terrapin were each captured at one site (Table 12). Northern diamond-backed terrapin was the only species captured in tidal marsh ditches (CR=0.8) and the eastern mud turtle was only captured in temporary pond habitat (CR=0.7) (Table 12). Dry conditions throughout much of the 2002 season made it difficult to effectively trap many sites, and traps were set even when sites contained little or no water in an effort to capture animals traveling through the wetlands.

Trapping in 2003 produced a total of 15 captures of eastern mud turtles, involving 12 unique individuals (Table 13). At Bigfoot pond, seven captures involved four individuals, one of which was captured three times and a second which was captured twice. This latter individual was the lone eastern mud turtle trapped at Bigfoot pond in 2002. Bellport Bay Ditches and Transect 4 Marsh each produced a total four captures involving four unique individuals. Two snapping turtles and 32 Fowler's toads were also captured (Table 13).

Minnow Trap Surveys
Minnow trap surveys at eight sites produced two species, Fowler's toad and American bullfrog. One Fowler's toad adult and 161 larvae were captured at Hospital Point Cranberry Bog. A single American bullfrog larvae was captured at Kismet Pond (Table 14). Dry conditions throughout much of the 2002 season made it difficult to effectively trap at some sites, and traps were set even when there was little or no water in an effort to capture animals traveling through the wetlands.

Table 11. Number of amphibians and reptiles recorded during coverboard surveys on Fire Island National Seashore, 2 April to 6 September 2002. Capture rate (in parentheses) is number recorded/100 board checks. Board checks are number of boards/site, multiplied by number of site visits. S= species richness= total # of species.

Site	Northern black racer	Fowler's toad	S	Boards/ Site	Site Visits	Board Checks	Boards with Snakes
Kismet CB Array 1			0	8	13	104	0
Kismet CB Array 2		1 (1.0)	1	8	13	104	0
SP to OI CB Array 1			0	8	9	72	0
SP to OI CB Array 2			0	8	9	72	0
OI to BB CB Array 3			0	8	8	64	0
OI to BB CB Array 4	1 (1.6)		1	8	8	64	1
Sailor's Haven CB Array 1	2 (2.3)		1	8*	12	87	1
Sailor's Haven CB Array 2		1 (1.0)	1	8	12	96	0
Sailor's Haven CB Array 3			0	8	12	96	0
Watch Hill CB Array 1			0	8	9	72	0
Watch Hill CB Array 2		1 (1.4)	1	8	9	72	0
Watch Hill CB Array 3			0	8	9	72	0
Total	3 (0.3)	3 (0.3)	2	96	123	975	2

*one board missing after 4/30/02

43

Table 12. Number of turtle captures in turtle traps on Fire Island National Seashore in 2002. Capture rate (in parentheses) is the number of captures per 100 trap nights.

Habitat	Site	First Date	Last Date	# of Traps	# of Trap Nights	# Captures			
						Snapping turtle	Spotted turtle	Eastern Mud turtle	Northern diamond-backed terrapin
Tidal marsh/ Swamp	Bellport Bay Ditches	7-May	7-Jun	5	40				1 (2.5)
	Hospital Point Ditches	7-May	7-Jun	5	40				
	Molasses Point Ditches	7-May	7-Jun	2	16				
	Watch Hill Ditches	30-Apr	31-May	4	32				
				Total	128	0	0	0	1 (0.8)
Non-tidal marsh	Molasses Point Marsh	7-May	7-Jun	1	8				
				Total	8				
Permanent pond	Kismet Pond	30-Apr	31-May	3 to 4	29	5 (17.2)			
	Sailor's Haven Maint. Pond	30-Apr	31-May	2	16				
				Total	45	5 (11.1)	0	0	0
Temporary pond	Bigfoot Pond	7-May	7-Jun	2	16			1 (6.3)	
	Sunken Forest Pond 2	30-Apr	31-May	2	16	1 (6.3)			
	Sunken Forest Pond 4	30-Apr	31-May	3	24	1 (4.2)			
	Sunken Forest Pond 6	30-Apr	31-May	3	24				
	Sunken Forest Pond 7	30-Apr	31-May	3	24	1 (4.2)			
	Watch Hill Boardwalk Pond	2-May	3-May	2	4				
	Watch Hill Pond 37	30-Apr	31-May	4 to 6	40		8 (20)		
				Total	148	3 (2.0)	8 (5.4)	1 (0.7)	0

44

Table 13. Number of turtle and anuran captures in turtle traps on Fire Island National Seashore in 2003. Capture rate (in parentheses) is the number of captures per 100 trap nights.

Site	First Date	Last Date	# of Traps	Water Depth (cm)	# of Trap Nights	# Captures		
						Eastern mud turtle	Snapping turtle	Fowler's toad
Bigfoot Pond	17-May	5-Jun	4 to 10	5 to 56	178	7 (3.9)		8 (4.5)
Transect 4 Marsh	19-May	4-Jun	8 to 10	11 to 45	166	4 (2.4)	1 (0.6)	5 (3.0)
Bellport Bay Ditches	18-May	4-Jun	8 to 16	5 to 20	272	4 (1.5)	1 (0.4)	19 (7.0)
Total					616	15 (2.4)	2 (0.3)	32 (5.2)

Table 14. Number of amphibian and reptile captures in minnow traps on Fire Island National Seashore, 2002. Capture rate (in parentheses) is the number of captures per 100 trap nights.

Habitat	Site	First Date	Last Date	# of Traps	# of Trap Nights	Fowler's toad adult	Fowler's toad larvae	American bullfrog larvae
Non-tidal marsh	Hospital Point Cranberry Bog	7-May	7-Jun	2	17	1 (5.9)	161 (947.1)	0
	Transect 4 Marsh	7-May	7-Jun	2	16			
				Total	33	1 (3.0)	161 (487.9)	0
Permanent pond	Kismet Pond	2-Apr	1-Aug	2 to 3	42			1 (2.4)
	Sailor's Haven Maintenance Pond	2-Apr	1-Aug	2	30			
				Total	72	0	0	1 (1.4)
Temporary pond	Sunken Forest Pond 2	2-Apr	1-Aug	2	28			
	Sunken Forest Pond 4	2-Apr	1-Aug	2 to 3	39			
	Sunken Forest Pond 6	2-Apr	1-Aug	2 to 3	39			
	Sunken Forest Pond 7	2-Apr	1-Aug	2 to 3	39			
				Total	145	0	0	0

Drift Fences

Four species were captured at the Kismet Pond drift fence. Fowler's toad dominated the catch, with 134 adults and 139 juveniles (metamorphs) (Table 15) and was found in traps all around the pond. Most adult Fowler's toads (81%) were captured between 27 March and 30 May and most juveniles (99%) were captured between 1 June and 22 August (Table 15). This is expected as adults migrate to the pond at the beginning of the season and juveniles disperse later, after metamorphosis. American bullfrog (7 adults and 3 juveniles) was the only other anuran captured. Snapping turtles (4 juveniles) and one eastern garter snake were the only reptiles captured (Table 15). Although no specific data were collected on precipitation, captures of amphibians generally coincided with periods of rain.

Incidental Encounters

Ten species were recorded as incidental encounters at 24 locations, 13 of which were also standardized survey sites. This includes two migratory species, a dead leatherback sea turtle washed up on the Point O'Woods Beach on 14 August 2002 and a dead loggerhead sea turtle washed up in Ocean Beach on 22 September 2002. A resident eastern hog-nosed snake, observed on May 14, 2007 at Watch Hill (ML Lamont, pers. comm.) is also included. Among the resident species, based on number of locations recorded, the most widespread species were Fowler's toad (16 locations), eastern box turtle (9 locations), and northern black racer and northern diamond-backed terrapin (5 locations each) (Table 16). Based on number of adult form individuals, the most abundant species was Fowler's toad (495 recorded), and the least abundant were eastern hog-nosed snake (1 recorded), and spotted turtle (3 recorded) (Table 16).

Table 15. Number of amphibian and reptile captures in drift-fence pitfall traps at Kismet Pond on Fire Island National Seashore, 27 March to 21 August 2002. Capture rate is number of captures per 100 trap nights.

Month	Species					
	Fowler's toad		American bullfrog		Snapping turtle	Eastern garter snake
	adult	juvenile	adult	juvenile	juvenile	adult
March/April	64		7	3	1	1
May	45	2				
June	16	23			3	
July/August	9	114				
Total	134	139	7	3	4	1
Capture Rate	2.89	3.00	0.15	0.06	0.09	0.02

Table 16. Number of amphibians and reptiles recorded as incidental encounters at 24 locations on Fire Island National Seashore, 2002-2003. Life stage or evidence of presence is: adl=adult; lrv=larvae; dor=dead on road; kll=kill; voc=anuran vocalization; shd=snake shed; nst=nest. Site total includes all evidence recorded, including an eastern hognose snake observed in May 2007.

Site	Fowler's toad adl	Fowler's toad voc	Snapping turtle adl	Snapping turtle adl	Eastern box Turtle shl	Spotted turtle adl	N. diamond-backed terrapin adl	N. diamond-backed terrapin shl	Leatherback sea turtle kll	Loggerhead sea turtle kll	Northern black racer adl	Northern black racer shd	Eastern hog-nosed snake nst	Eastern hog-nosed snake adl	Eastern garter snake adl	Eastern garter snake dor	Site Total
Bellport Bay (S)	2	70						1									73
Bigfoot Pond (S)	7	37			1												45
Bellport Beach to Old Inlet (bayside) (S)								1									1
Bellport Beach to Old Inlet (interior) (S)	2						1	1			5	1	2				12
Hospital Point Ditches (S)		6						1									7
Kismet Interior (S)	10		3	2							2				2	2	21
Lonelyville (IE)	1																1
Molasses Point Marsh (S)	1	76															77
Ocean Bay Park (IE)			1														1
Ocean Beach (IE)										1							1
Old Inlet Marsh (IE)	3	37															40
OPWA (IE)	3	140															143
Point O'Woods (IE)	8								1					1			10
Sailor's Haven (IE)	2				2												4

Site	Fowler's toad (adl)	Fowler's toad (voc)	Snapping turtle (adl)	Eastern box turtle (adl)	Eastern box turtle (shl)	Spotted turtle (adl)	N. diamond-backed terrapin (adl)	N. diamond-backed terrapin (shl)	Leatherback sea turtle (kll)	Loggerhead sea turtle (kll)	Northern black racer (adl)	Northern black racer (shd)	Northern black racer (nst)	Eastern hog-nosed snake (adl)	Eastern garter snake (adl)	Eastern garter snake (dor)	Site Total
Saltaire (IE)	1																1
Old Inlet to Smith Point (bayside) (S)							1	2									3
Old Inlet to Smith Point (interior) (S)	1										1						2
Sunken Forest (S)	4	2	2	2		1					3						14
Sunken Forest Carex Marsh (IE)	1	35															36
Sunken Forest Pond 5 (IE)				1													1
Sunken Forest Pond 7 (S)				1													1
Sunken Forest Pond 8 (S)				1													1
Watch Hill (IE)	11	35	3								1			1			51
Watch Hill Boardwalk Pond (S)						2											2
Species Total	57	438	8	9	3	3	2	6	1	1	12	1	2	1	2	2	548
Total # of Sites	16		3	9	3	2	5	5	1	1	5		2	1	1	2	24

Discussion

Community Composition

The 10 resident species recorded on FIIS are a small portion of the 38 species of amphibians and reptiles native to and resident on Long Island (Noble 1927), but comprise nearly all the resident species that likely occurred on FIIS historically (Appendix A). One species known to have occurred historically, the southern leopard frog (Overton 1914) is no longer present, and one species currently present, the American Bullfrog, is likely a recent arrival. Its presence on FIIS was first noted ca.1999 at Kismet pond (S. Finn, pers. comm.), and, for reasons that will be discussed below, it is likely that this population is the result of a recent release, rather than a historically-occurring population or recent natural colonization. Thus, the current herpetofauna of FIIS consists of 9 of 10 of the known historically-occurring species, plus one recent arrival.

Barrier islands typically have low herpetofaunal species richness due to reduced habitat diversity and environmental stressors (Mitchell and Anderson 1994). The low species richness of FIIS is not surprising and is the result of several factors. These include the pool of species available to colonize and their dispersal abilities, the connectivity between Fire Island and Long Island, and habitat availability on Fire Island. Long Island is geologically young, formed of glacial moraine and outwash plains, and was only briefly connected to the continental mainland prior to sea level rise since the last glacial retreat (Pough and Pough 1968). Because of its recent creation and insular nature, Long Island lacks several species of vertebrates found on the adjacent mainland (Noble 1927, Connor 1971). Species richness is further reduced on Long Island's outwash plain (Noble 1926), which extends southward from the terminal moraines down to Long Island's south shore. Based on a comprehensive review of historic literature and museum specimens, Cook (in prep.), estimated that 31 species of amphibians and reptiles likely occurred historically along the south shore of Long Island. Among these 31 species, there are six salamanders, nine anurans, six turtles, and 10 snakes.

Geologically, Fire Island is far younger than Long Island, with its major development within the last 3000 years (Psuty et al, 2005, pers. comm.). Based on a number of maps dating from the 1600's to the present (e.g. Bien 1895), it appears the present-day Fire Island was a barrier peninsula or island that extended west from a base in close contact with the Long Island "mainland", with the continuity of the peninsula changing as the inlets through this spit came and went. Although it varied over time during this period, the east end of the peninsula was very close to the "mainland" and sometimes connected at Mastic, Quogue, Westhampton, and/or Southampton, whereas, to the west, distance over water between the island and the "mainland" increased. During this time, small land animals would have been able to colonize overland and/or across short distances of salt marsh at the island's east end and, given appropriate habitat, work their way west until blocked by an inlet. However, as inlets closed, they would have been able to advance further west, allowing them to eventually extend the length of the barrier, which itself was slowly elongating westward (Psuty et al. 2005). Since the creation and maintenance of the Moriches Inlet in 1938 (and the intra-coastal waterway), however, that process no longer occurs, and Fire Island is now much more isolated from potential colonizers.

51

Reptiles are better colonizers of barrier islands than amphibians, and among amphibians, anurans are much better than salamanders (Gibbons and Coker 1978). Further, since population establishment on an island not only requires overcoming dispersal barriers but also finding appropriate habitat, given the significant positive correlation between species richness and amount of woodland habitat, particularly for amphibians (Gibbons and Coker 1978), the limited amount of woodland habitat on Fire Island is yet another factor limiting species richness. Thus, the herpetofauna of FIIS consists of the relatively few species, primarily reptiles, that were capable of successfully dispersing onto the peninsula/island, taking advantage of its relatively limited habitat, and surviving in the environmental conditions associated with barrier islands, such as ocean overwash, limited freshwater habitat, limited cover, and extended periods of dry conditions.

Although amphibians numerically dominated the herpetofauna recorded, accounting for 88% of individuals recorded, in terms of species richness, reptiles dominated, accounting for 80% (8/10) of resident species recorded. Dominance of species richness by reptiles is typical of barrier spits and islands and reflects both their higher tolerance of salt and xeric conditions, limited habitats present, and generally less complex life cycle (Mitchell and Andersen 1994). The dominance of resident species richness by reptiles on FIIS is similar to that observed at Sandy Hook, NJ, a nearby barrier spit where 89% (8/9) of species currently present are reptiles (Cook, in prep).

With one exception, the herpetofaunal community of FIIS is composed of species typical of Northeastern barrier islands. Among the amphibians, toads (*Bufo* sp.) are widespread on barrier islands (Gibbons and Coker 1978). Fowler's toad is the typical toad of the Northeast coast (Klemens 1993) and the only species of *Bufo* native to Long Island. It is well known as a salt and desiccation-tolerant species, which accounts for it being recorded in greater numbers and from more locations than any other species in this survey (Tables 2, 3). In contrast, American bullfrogs, although common on Long Island, were not typically found along the south shore (Noble 1926, Yeaton 1974) and are not generally found on barrier islands (Gibbons and Coker 1978). These facts further support the idea they were introduced to FIIS. Of the snakes, both the hog-nosed snake and black racer were once common and widespread along Long Island's south shore and barrier islands (Engelhardt et al. 1915, Murphy 1950, Smith 1963) and the Eastern garter snake is a ubiquitous and common species. Similarly, the non-marine turtles present on FIIS are species that are or were once widespread (snapping turtle, eastern box turtle, spotted turtle) and/or coastal/salt marsh specialists in the region (Eastern Mud Turtle, Northern Diamond-backed Terrapin).

Important Sites and Habitats

The "importance" of sites and/or habitats can be approached from a number of perspectives, such as species richness, numbers of individuals, or importance to particular species such as keystone species or rare or "listed" species. From a resident species richness perspective, species richness on FIIS was equal in wetlands and uplands (9 species). The most species rich habitats were beachgrass/beach heather/low thicket (7 species), tidal marsh/swamp (6 species), and temporary pond, holly/mixed forest, and developed, each with five resident species recorded (Table 2). Individual sites with high resident species richness were Kismet Interior and Sunken Forest, each with five species, and Kismet Pond, Watch Hill, Bellport Bay, and Old Inlet to Bellport Bay, with four species each (Table 4). However, although amphibians and reptiles commonly utilize

52

specific habitats one part of the year, they often require different habitats for breeding, foraging, dispersal, and/or hibernation. For example, Fowler's toads, spotted and mud turtles depart wetlands following the breeding season, foraging, hibernating and aestivating in surrounding open, sandy uplands (Ernst et al. 1994; Conant and Collins 1998). Female snapping turtles and diamond-backed terrapins migrate to uplands in the late spring to nest in open areas with loose, sandy soil, and eastern box turtles will enter wetlands for up to several weeks at a time during warm summer months (Ernst et al. 1994; Donaldson and Echternacht 2005).

Because of these complex life cycles, what is more important than any single habitat type is a landscape that provides all the necessary habitat elements, in sufficient quantity and degree of interspersion to allow animals to safely move among them. Given this, and the island's narrow, linear nature, fragmentation by private development and high degree of habitat interspersion, a more useful perspective may be to look at tracts. From this perspective, the most important tracts are the adjacent Watch Hill and OPWA. There were six resident species recorded in each (Table 5), and if considered as a single tract, which makes more sense ecologically, this tract had 8 of 10 resident species present. This includes both wide ranging species, such as Fowler's toad, snapping turtle, box turtle, and black racer, plus more restricted species, such as diamond-backed terrapin, eastern mud turtle, spotted turtle, and eastern hog-nosed snake. Of these latter four, three of which are "listed" species, all or nearly all individuals recorded in this survey were in this combined tract. Moreover, all four of the New York State "listed" species found on FIIS during this survey (and 56.6% of all individuals of these four species) were recorded from this tract, which also accounted for 44.2% of total individuals recorded (516/1168). This tract's importance derives from it being the largest on the island, with a relatively greater width, which has allowed for development of many temporary freshwater wetlands, plus extensive salt marsh habitat on the bay side as well.

Sailor's Haven is another important tract, with five species and 12.5% of all individuals recorded. This tract, particularly the Sunken Forest area, accounted for 75% of all Eastern box turtles recorded (Table 5), as well as a spotted turtle and wider ranging species such as Fowler's toad, snapping turtle, and black racer. Although there were six species and 31.9% of all individuals recorded from the Lighthouse tract, four of these were wide-ranging species on the island, Fowler's toad, snapping turtle, box turtle, and black racer. The other two species were only recorded within this tract, but one of them, American bullfrog, was likely a recent introduction to Kismet Pond, and the other, eastern garter snake, is the most common and widespread snake in the northeast (Klemens 1993).

Species at Risk
Most of the 10 species of resident amphibians and reptiles recently documented on FIIS are widespread in North America and were once common in the Northeast (Conant and Collins 1998; Klemens 1993). However, several are now declining in this region and four are New York State "listed" species. These four are the eastern mud turtle (NY *Endangered*), and three *Special Concern* species, eastern hog-nosed snake, spotted turtle, and eastern box turtle. As detailed in species accounts below, their declines are due to a number of factors, mostly related to development, habitat fragmentation, pollution, over-collecting, and road kill (NYDEC 2000). From a preservation of "species at risk" perspective, FIIS is a critical site for New York State mud turtles. FIIS is one of only six sites in the state where this NY *Endangered*) species is

known to occur (Breisch and Ozard, in prep). For the three *Special Concern* species, FIIS is one of many sites where these species have been recently recorded (Breisch and Ozard, in prep). Box turtles have declined throughout much of their range due to habitat loss, fragmentation, suburbanization and road kill (Dodd 2001) and are declining on Long Island (Gibbs et al. 2007). The same factors also affect spotted turtles and eastern hog-nosed snakes, and their populations on Long Island have also declined (Smith 1963, Yeaton 1974, Schlauch 1976). In addition, although not formally listed, the black racer has also declined dramatically on Long Island (Schlauch 1976) and is declining in New York State (Gibbs et al. 2007). It typically occurs in open habitats and requires fairly large patches of habitat (Kjoss and Litvaitis 2001). Similarly, Fowler's toad, though once considered to be very tolerant of suburbanization on Long Island (Schlauch 1976), is now declining in the Northeast as suburbanization intensifies and open habitats succeed into woodlands (Tupper and Cook 2008). Because these six species do not fare well on the increasingly fragmented and suburbanized landscape of Long Island, FIIS, with its large, effectively roadless tracts and diverse mix of habitats, provides a regionally important site where these species have a real chance for long term persistence.

Population Trends

Determining population trends on FIIS is difficult, given the extremely limited historical data. As detailed above, there have been no prior attempts to broadly sample Fire Island's amphibians and reptiles, and the "historic" data on species occurrence (Overton 1914; Murphy 1950; Smith 1962, 1963; Yeaton 1974; Northup 1986; Meyer 1988; Barcia 1996; Caldecutt 1997; Klemens 1997; Williamson 1999; Putnam 1999) is very piecemeal. In spite of these limitations, some of these sources do provide a qualitative sense of abundance for some species. In conjunction with current data and a sense of habitat suitability and species detectability, we have attempted to assess each species' status and population trends

Based on this somewhat subjective approach, it appears that of 10 resident species historically present, seven appear to be stable in terms of their population trends. Of the remaining three, Fowler's toad may be less common, or at the least underwent a decline in recent decades from which it has mostly recovered. The eastern hog-nosed snake has declined to the point of being extremely rare and another, the southern leopard frog has been extirpated (Table 17). In addition, one species, the American bullfrog, has increased, in the sense that it was not likely a part of the "historic" herpetofauna of FIIS and has been introduced.

Table 17. "Historic" status and apparent trends in resident amphibians and reptiles on FIIS. *not recorded in 2002-2003,**recorded in 2007.

Common Name	Historic Status	Current Status	Apparent Trend
Fowler's toad	abundant	common	slight decline
Southern leopard frog*	abundant	extirpated	decline
American bullfrog	not present	uncommon	increase
Snapping turtle	common	common	stable
Eastern mud turtle	common	uncommon	decline
Spotted turtle	common	uncommon	decline
Northern diamond-backed terrapin	common	common	stable
Eastern box turtle	common	common	stable
Northern black racer	common	common	stable
Eastern hog-nosed snake**	abundant	rare	decline
Eastern garter snake	unknown	uncommon	stable

Stressors

The natural environment of barrier beaches is inherently stressful to organisms (Mitchell and Anderson 1994) and on FIIS natural stressors include geographic isolation, ocean overwash and storm surge, limited freshwater habitat, limited cover, and extended periods of dry conditions. These limit the species capable of successfully colonizing a barrier island such as FIIS, make random, localized population extinctions more likely, and successful re-colonization afterwards less likely. Added to these are anthropogenic stressors, which may be global or more localized. Global stressors tend to affect large geographic areas, often far removed from their ultimate cause or source, and include ultraviolet-B radiation and atmospherically transported pollutants such as mercury and acid rain. Stressors such as other heavy metals, chemicals found in fertilizers, herbicides, and pesticides, habitat degradation, disease, road mortality, and introduced species (Dunson et al. 1992, Blaustein 1994, Blaustein et al. 1994, Pechman and Wilbur 1994, Hunter et al. 1999, Daszak et al. 2000, Knapp and Matthews 2000) may also be widespread in their scope, but tend to be more variable across the landscape in their extent and effects. Thus their impacts may be at either a regional or local level.

A number of these global or regional stressors are known to occur on FIIS. Mercury is transported atmospherically and deposited, often far from the source, and can be accumulated by aquatic organisms to the point of causing lethal or sub-lethal effects. Mercury deposition occurs throughout the Northeast, and even aquatic systems of relatively undeveloped areas such as Acadia National Park (Bank et al. 2006) and Cape Cod National Seashore contain high levels of mercury. The problem occurs when low pH, in part due to acid rain, leads to elevated concentrations of mercury. This process has been linked to the decline of northern dusky salamanders at Acadia NP (Bank et al. 2006) and elevated, but non-lethal levels in snapping turtles (Golet and Haines 2001). Research elsewhere has shown that increased mercury levels increase abnormalities and mortality in larval southern leopard frogs (Unrine et al. 2004). Given that both acid precipitation and mercury deposition occurs in the vicinity of FIIS (Kroenke et al. 2003, NY S DEC 2008) it is reasonable to conclude that FIIS is subjected to inputs from both of these stressors, but we are not aware of any data on mercury levels or impacts to biota at FIIS.

Pesticides are another stressor present on FIIS. DDT was sprayed extensively and indiscriminately to control mosquitoes in Suffolk County wetlands and grasslands for 15 years, ending in 1966, and many marine invertebrates in Great South Bay were locally extirpated (Jankowski 2004). Although quantities are unknown, DDT was applied to Fire Island marshes during this period (Flora et al. 1992). At present, a number of pesticides targeted at mosquitoes are applied on Fire Island, primarily within the private communities. Since current applications in the private communities include aerial spraying, these pesticides likely affect organisms on NPS property (Jankowski 2004).

Although these stressors are well known to be present on FIIS, little is known with certainty of their impacts to the island's herpetofauna. In general, these stressors tend to adversely affect amphibians more than reptiles, and mercury primarily affects wholly aquatic species. The inherent paucity of amphibians on FIIS meant there were few species present to be affected by these contaminants, yet it is likely that one or a combination of them are responsible for the extirpation of southern leopard frogs on FIIS. Whether there were any impacts to Fowler's toad is unknown, but DDT spraying is responsible for eliminating populations of Fowler's toad on several small islands off the coast of Cape Cod (Lazell 1976) and probably also at Sandy Hook, NJ (Cook, in prep). Although speculative, the decline of hog-nosed snakes, a once abundant species on Fire Island that feeds almost exclusively on Fowler's toad, is hard to attribute to habitat loss or human persecution and seems more likely to be the result of a crash in the Fowler's toad population from which the hog-nosed snake has yet to recover. Some combination of pesticides and/or mercury effects seem to be the most plausible explanation.

More localized stressors, such as road kill and continued development and habitat fragmentation, are not operating to any great extent on FIIS, but they likely exert some influence by preventing further natural colonization or re-colonization. Habitat loss and fragmentation along Long Island's south shore also means there are fewer source populations available. In addition dredged channels now separate Fire Island from the mainland, and the Moriches inlet is maintained, making it unlikely that individuals from remnant populations on the "mainland" would be able to get to Fire Island naturally. Thus, any extirpations, such as has occurred to the southern leopard frog, are unlikely to be reversed by natural recolonization. Another likely stressor, although unknown in terms of its extent, is collection. Both box turtles and spotted turtles are frequently kept as pets and sold, and it is possible that some collection is occurring. Conversely, the release of animals from off-island is also occurring, as evidenced by the recent appearance of bullfrogs at Kismet Pond. Box turtles, although a native species on FIIS, are probably also being released in small numbers, as animals kept as pets are released or wild animals are rescued from harm's way and relocated to safety. The release of animals on Fire Island poses dangers such as disease introduction to native species and disruption of native communities in the event that a non-native species became established. Thus, although FIIS does provide important, undeveloped habitat far removed from many of the stressors impacting amphibians and reptiles on mainland Long Island, there are still a number of threats present and the continued persistence of the species currently present should not be taken for granted.

Summation
Because of geographic isolation, limited freshwater habitat, and harsh environmental conditions, FIIS has few species of amphibians and reptiles compared to Long Island (19 amphibian, 19

reptile). Of the 10 resident species known to have occurred historically on FIIS, nine were recently documented by this survey. Of these 10 species, seven appear to be stable in terms of their population trends. Of the remaining three, Fowler's toad may be less common, or at the least underwent a decline in recent decades from which it has mostly recovered. The eastern hog-nosed snake has declined to the point of being extremely rare and the southern leopard frog has been extirpated. Thus, the naturally-depauperate herpetofauna of FIIS has been further reduced by the loss of at least one species, likely due to pesticides or other contaminants. In spite of these limitations, FIIS is an important site for herpetofauna, especially reptiles. Four of the resident species present are listed by New York State as either *Endangered* (eastern mud turtle) or *Special Concern* (eastern box turtle, spotted turtle, eastern hog-nosed snake). Because many of the stressors that are negatively impacting these species regionally do not operate on FIIS, populations within the park are relatively well protected, and FIIS plays an important role in helping to preserve the region's herpetofaunal diversity.

While a detailed plan for monitoring is beyond the scope of this inventory, the results suggest that a program based on anuran calling surveys, time or spatially constrained surveys, turtle trapping, and monitoring freshwater wetland water quality would be the most useful for generating quantitative data for trends analysis. Further work on eastern mud turtle, spotted turtle, eastern box turtle, and eastern-hog-nosed snake should also be a high priority.

Species Accounts

Fowler's Toad (Bufo fowleri)

Fowler's toad is widespread in the eastern U.S., and in the Northeast is found mostly along the coastal plain, extending inland up river valleys (Klemens 1993). Fowler's toads are primarily terrestrial, foraging and hibernating on land and migrating to wetlands to breed. They are habitat specialists found primarily in sparsely vegetated, sandy areas (Breden 1988) and breed in both permanent and temporary freshwater wetlands, avoiding those with a canopy of woody vegetation (Tupper and Cook, 2008).

Historically, Fowler's toad was common and widespread in the New York Metropolitan area (Noble 1927) and, although similar to and sometimes hybridizing with the American toad (*Bufo americanus*), was known to be the only species of toad (i.e. *Bufo*) found on Long Island (Overton 1914). Although they were negatively impacted by urbanization in NYC by the mid-20th century (Kieran 1959), their relatively simple life cycle, ability to breed in various wetlands, including temporary and human-created ones, and to forage in suburban yards made Fowler's toad one of the most "urban tolerant" of Long Island amphibians (Schlauch 1976). However, throughout the Northeast U.S., Fowler's toad is now becoming less common due to habitat loss, pesticides (Lazell 1976), and hydrologic alterations (Tupper et al. 2007).

Previous surveys on FIIS suggested that Fowler's toad was the most common and widespread species in the park (Northup 1986; Caldecutt 1997; Klemens 1997; Putnam 1999) and our results show its status in this regard remains the same. The Fowler's toad was the most frequently recorded species in this survey, with 1002 adults recorded from 33 localities (FO=67.3%) in all habitat types (Tables 2 and 3). A plurality of individuals recorded were from permanent ponds (34.0%), but this species bred in all wetland types (Table 2), and adults were heard calling from wetlands the entire length of the island. Consistent with it being a terrestrial species outside of the breeding season, adults were also frequently observed traveling over the sand in grass and along dirt roads in the park, especially during and after periods of rain.

In spite of Fowler's toad continuing to be the most common and widespread species on FIIS, there are a number of anecdotal reports (e.g. H. Ginsberg, pers. comm.), plus additional circumstantial evidence, suggesting it is not as abundant as in the past, or at the least, underwent a significant decline at some point in recent decades. Although an apparent decline based on anecdotal reports is weak and inconclusive, the dramatic decline of the hog-nosed snake on Fire Island (Yeaton 1974, Putnam 1999) suggests that the population of Fowler's toads on Fire Island has not been consistently abundant. Because Fowler's toads are the almost exclusive prey of hog-nosed snakes, dramatic declines in toad populations lead to the same in hog-nosed snakes. The loss of Fowler's toad populations at Sandy Hook and Breezy Point at Gateway NRA, leading to local extirpation of hog-nosed snakes there are two examples (Cook, in prep). Although, habitat loss and human persecution are two other common factors in the local decline of hog-nosed snakes (Smith 1963), these factors have not operated that intensely on Fire Island. DDT-related declines in hog-nosed snakes, via endocrine disruption, might also be a factor but applications of DDT sufficient to affect a snake would likely have an even greater impact on an amphibian, due to their more permeable skin (Henry 2000). Thus, the dramatic decline of hog-nosed snakes on FIIS seems likely to be the result of a temporary crash in the Fowler's toad population due to pesticides. Although the Fowler's toad population may have already passed through this "bottleneck", it appears the hog-nosed snake has yet to recover.

Southern Leopard Frog (*Rana sphenocephala*)

The southern leopard frog is widespread through the south central and southeast United States, except for Appalachia, and ranges northward along the Atlantic coastal plain to the lower Hudson River valley and Long Island (Conant and Collins 1998). Considered to be one of the most common frogs throughout most of its range, southern leopard frogs breed in shallow marshes and are otherwise found in a broad range of riverine and wetland habitats, including salt marshes (Butterfield et al. 2005, Gibbs et al. 2007). Although southern New York State is the northern limit of their distribution, southern leopard frogs were abundant historically along the coastal marshes of the New York Metropolitan area (Ditmars 1905, Noble 1927). Overton (1914) considered this species to be especially common on the salt marshes of Long Island's south shore and abundant on Fire Island, which he refers to by its older name, "Great South Beach".

Southern leopard frogs are now listed as a Special Concern Species in New York State and recent efforts to locate extant populations on Long Island have not been successful (J. Feinberg, pers. comm.). Yeaton (1968) noted they were common at a number of sites along the south shore, from Islip to Old Mastic, and they were still abundant in Bridgehampton in the 1980's (Nelson 2005). Feinberg et al. (2007) state their decline on Long Island occurred "over the past 30 to 50 years", essentially beginning in the late 1950's. Exactly when they declined on Fire Island is uncertain, but they are not included on a 1972 Faunal List (Rozsa 1972, R. Rozsa pers. comm), nor have there been any reported in the park's history. Reasons for the apparent extirpation of southern leopard frogs on Long Island are uncertain, but likely include habitat loss, fragmentation, invasion by *Phragmites*, environmental contaminants, and disease (J. Feinberg, pers. comm.). On FIIS, their extirpation is probably more likely due to pesticides, disease, and/or mercury than habitat loss and fragmentation.

American Bullfrog (*Rana catesbeiana*)

The American bullfrog is a widespread and common species throughout much of North America, and is found throughout New York, including Long Island (NYDEC 2000; Conant and Collins 1998). Bullfrogs require two or more years for their tadpoles to metamorphose, hence it occurs primarily in open bodies of water such as lakes and ponds (Conant and Collins 1998). Their primary habitat requirement is a permanent water body with abundant emergent and shoreline vegetation (Hunter et al. 1999). This species is an aggressive predator that includes other frogs, young turtles, small snakes, and many invertebrates in its diet. It is adept at colonizing new habitats, especially those constructed or modified by humans (Lacki et al.1992) and, because it is primarily aquatic, is relatively urban tolerant (Klemens 1993).

Historically, the American bullfrog has been widespread and common in the New York metropolitan area (Ditmars 1905, Noble 1927) although Overton (1914) commented that they had declined on Long Island. Their original distribution and greatest abundance on Long Island appears to have been primarily in freshwater ponds associated with the terminal moraine (Noble 1927, Yeaton 1968) rather than the outwash plain. However, damming of streams for mill ponds greatly increased the amount of permanent freshwater pond habitat on Long Island (Schlauch 1976), particularly along the south shore, and bullfrogs now occur extensively there as well (Breisch and Ozard, in prep). On FIIS, the American bullfrog was only recorded at Kismet Pond, where it is common (30 adults and 5 larvae recorded; Tables 2 and 6). Kismet Pond is the only large, permanent pond on the island (Sailor's Haven pond is much smaller and shallow). Given the lack of suitable habitat (permanent freshwater pond), it is unlikely to be found elsewhere on the island.

The American bullfrog tends to be conspicuous where it occurs and the lack of any records of this species on FIIS until very recently (Putnam 1999; Steve Finn pers. comm.) suggests it is a recent arrival (late 1990's). Given the island's present isolation, reinforced by the dredged channels of the intra-coastal waterway and Moriches inlet, and the lack of any habitat for this species to the east (the end of the island that originally connected to the mainland), it is unlikely that this species arrived at Kismet Pond naturally. Bullfrogs are not generally found on barrier islands (Gibbons and Coker 1978), and their recent arrival at Kismet pond, on the heavily-visited, motor vehicle accessible west end of the island, appears to be a case of an unauthorized release. When introduced to areas where they are not native, bullfrogs can displace native species (Adams 1999; Stumpel 1992), and their tadpoles may dramatically alter aquatic community structure (Kupferberg 1994). In this case however, given their restricted range on the island and the paucity of other amphibian species on Fire Island to interact with, the capacity for this non-native population of bullfrogs to impact the native community of amphibians and reptiles is limited.

Snapping Turtle *(Chelydra serpentina)*

The snapping turtle occurs from southern Canada, south through the mid-west and east coast, down to Florida and the Gulf of Mexico (Ernst et al. 1994). It is abundant and widespread in New York State (Gibbs et al., 2007) and New England (Klemens 1993), and is the largest freshwater turtle in the northeastern United States. Although snapping turtles occur in nearly all freshwater habitats and also in brackish marshes, adults tend to occur more frequently in permanent water bodies and are most abundant in shallow, muddy ones (Klemens 1993; Cook et al. 2007). Typical of all turtles, eggs are laid on land. Female snapping turtles must emerge from wetlands and travel overland in search of nesting areas, generally open, sandy, sparsely vegetated patches (Gibbs et al. 2007). They are often seen crossing roads in late spring-early summer. Females dig nests and deposit eggs in loose sand or soil, and the hatchlings emerge in the late summer or early fall (Ernst et al. 1994).

Historically, snapping turtles were considered widespread and common throughout the NYC Metropolitan area (Engelhardt 1913; Murphy 1916; Noble 1927). Because urbanization has created additional permanent ponds in the NYC-Long Island region (Schlauch 1976) and snapping turtles are largely aquatic, primarily nocturnal, and tolerant of water pollution, they are able to survive urbanization (Klemens 1985) and are widespread in and around New York City (Kieran 1959) and Long Island (Breisch and Ozard in prep).

Northup (1986) considered snapping turtles to be rare on FIIS, due to a lack of permanent freshwater ponds on the island. In this survey, however, they were tied for #1 in ranked abundance among turtles, with 25 individuals recorded. Snapping turtles were recorded from

10 sites (FO=20.4%), in all habitat types, with the permanent freshwater Kismet pond and adjacent uplands being the single most important site, accounting for nearly half (12/25) of all records (Tables 2, 3, 4, Appendix D). Searches and trapping in the Sunken Forest and associated ponds provided the first records of this species in the Sunken Forest, with five snapping turtles (20% of all snapping turtles) (Table 4). In addition, snapping turtles were previously recorded from several freshwater and brackish water wetlands in the Bellport Bay Ditches, Watch Hill, OPWA, and the Fire Island Pines (Meyer 1988; Barcia 1996; Caldecutt 1997; Putnam 1999) Even though only two permanent ponds are found on FIIS, these records collectively indicate the snapping turtle has successfully utilized those ponds, along with the other various temporary pond and tidal marsh habitats, and actually is a common species here. Moreover, the size distribution of individuals recorded, from recent hatchlings to large adults (Figure 15), with 14 of 23 individuals juvenile (i.e. not sexually mature; Appendix D), suggests a viable population.

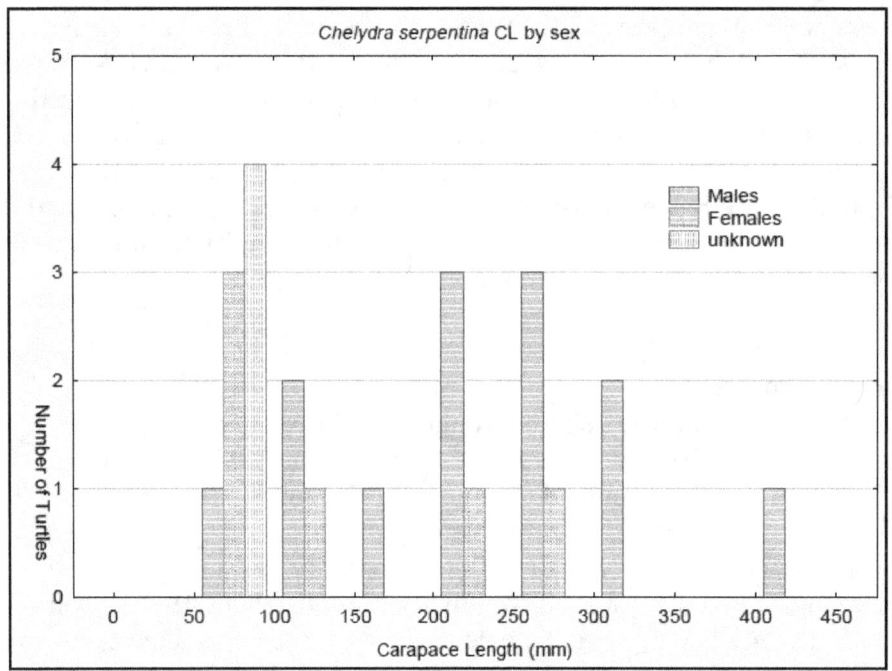

Figure 15. Frequency distribution of snapping turtles (*Chelydra serpentina*) by size and sex on FIIS, 2002 and 2003.

Loggerhead Sea Turtle (*Caretta caretta*)

The loggerhead sea turtle is the largest hard-shelled turtle, reaching three to four feet carapace length and weighing 300 to 500 pounds when mature. The species is widely distributed in the Pacific, Indian and Atlantic Oceans and Caribbean and Mediterranean Seas. On the Atlantic coast of North America, it nests primarily from Florida to South Carolina, and rarely as far north as southern New Jersey (Ernst et al. 1994). Loggerheads are one of five species of marine turtles found in the Atlantic Ocean that migrate north to feed as ocean temperatures increase in the summer. They occur in the open ocean, and also in Long Island Sound, Peconic Bay, and Great South Bay (Morreale et al. 1992; Shoop and Kenney 1992). This species occasionally succumbs to natural cold stunning, after sudden drops in temperature, generally from November through March, but the vast majority of these individuals are found in Long Island Sound and Peconic

Bay (Meylan and Sadove 1986; Morreale et al. 1992). A severely decomposed juvenile loggerhead washed up on Ocean Beach on 22 September 2002. Due to advanced decomposition, the Riverhead Foundation for Marine Research and Preservation was unable to say much about cause of death. The loggerhead is listed as a state and federally *Threatened* species. Although they occur in the waters of Fire Island, dead and/or cold stunned individual only occasionally wash ashore, and the occurrence of the loggerhead sea turtle on the beaches of FIIS is uncommon.

Leatherback Sea Turtle *(Dermochelys coriacea)*

The leatherback sea turtle ranges around the world from the Atlantic to the Pacific to the Indian Oceans (NYDEC 2000) and feeds primarily on oceanic jellyfish (Scyphomedusae). As a seasonal migrant to the North Atlantic they are found off the coast of Massachusetts and the Gulf of Maine, in Long Island waters, in the Gulf of Mexico, as well as along the shores of Canada, the British Isles, Iceland, Europe and Spain (NYDEC 2000). A counter-current circulatory system allows the leatherback to maintain a core body temperature in excess of the ocean water's (Lazell 1976) and consequently, leatherbacks tend to migrate further north than other marine turtles (Shoop and Kenney 1992). This huge marine turtle measures from five to eight feet, 1500 to 2000 pounds when mature, and has a brown to black, smooth, elongated, lyre-shaped carapace that tapers to a point above the tail (Ernst et al. 1994). One dead adult leatherback sea turtle measuring approximately five feet in length and 600 pounds washed up on the Point O'Woods Beach on 14 August 2002. A necropsy performed by the Riverhead Foundation discovered a latex balloon in the esophagus of the turtle. Leatherback sea turtles will mistake trash such as plastic bags and latex balloons for jellyfish, and this can contribute to gastrointestinal complications and death (Ernst et al. 1994). The leatherback is listed as a state and federally *Endangered* species. Although they occur in the waters of Fire Island, dead and/or cold stunned individual only occasionally wash ashore and the occurrence of the leatherback sea turtle on the beaches of FIIS is uncommon.

Eastern Mud Turtle *(Kinosternon subrubrum subrubrum)*

The eastern mud turtle is a small aquatic turtle with a smooth, dark olive to black oval carapace, a double-hinged plastron, and 11 marginal scutes rather than the 12 found on most turtles. Its diet includes crayfish, mollusks, beetles, insects, and amphibians. Mud turtles are typically found in shallow muddy wetlands with soft bottoms and abundant aquatic vegetation and, along the coast, are also found in salt marshes and brackish ponds dominated by *Phragmites* (Ernst et al. 1994; Gibbs et al. 2007). Mud turtles can be quite terrestrial and utilize uplands for both nesting and hibernation. The eastern mud turtle ranges from Mississippi eastward through the southeastern United States and northern Florida, and then northward through the coastal states, with its northern limit reached on Long Island, NY (Conant and Collins 1998). In the New York Metropolitan area, mud turtles occur on Long Island, Staten Island and along coastal New Jersey.

Historically, mud turtles were considered widespread and common in the region, especially on the coastal plain (Noble 1927). Engelhardt (1913) noted they were common in streams and ponds in Brooklyn, and they also occurred in the salt marshes on the south shore of Staten Island and Long Island (Murphy 1916; Leng and Davis 1930), including East Patchogue and Mastic, where it was frequently seen (Nichols 1914). Wetland alteration and development, road kill, industrial development and road construction have led to declines in New York mud turtle populations

(NYDEC 2000; Gibbs et al. 2007) and they are listed as *Endangered* in New York State. Locally, the Moriches inlet, created by the Hurricane of 1938 and artificially maintained through dredging since, has led to increased salinity in Moriches Bay and eastern Great South Bay, and appears to have played a role in the mud turtle's decline in this area (Nichols 1947). Only a handful of isolated populations (six) now remain in New York, one on Staten Island, and others in Patchogue, Fire Island and eastern Long Island (Breisch and Ozard in prep).

Long documented from East Patchogue and Mastic on the mainland side (Murphy 1916) and listed as occurring on Fire Island without any details provided by McCormick (1975), the first known documentation of eastern mud turtle on Fire Island seems to be from 1986 (Meyer 1988). Trapping and searching in the Bellport Bay Ditches in June 1988 (10 June to 29 June) resulted in the capture of 12 individuals. Including two individuals with multiple captures, there were a total of 15 captures during this period, which included 380 trap nights and an unspecified amount of time spent searching daily. Nine captures were by hand and six in traps (CR traps=1.6 captures/100 trap night). Follow-up searches in 1989 (three occasions) and in 1990 ("several" occasions) resulted in three captures and three individuals, one of which as an animal initially captured in 1988. Thus, during this period (1988-1990) there were a total 14 unique individuals captured (9 adult and 5 juvenile) and 18 capture events (12 hand and 6 trap) (Meyer 1988).

Follow-up trapping and searching was conducted by NPS volunteers and seasonal staff through most of the 1990's. According to notes and reports from FIIS files (e.g. Barcia 1995, Williamson 1999) trapping and searches for mud turtles were conducted in 1993, 94, 95, 96, and 1999, primarily in the Bellport Bay Ditches during May, June, and July. These accounts lack details of sampling effort, but indicate that effort generally consisted of four traps checked daily, and suggest that sampling in any given year extended over a two month period. No mud turtles were captured in the Bellport Bay Ditches during this period, but, in response to a sight record (Caldecutt 1997) one mud turtle was trapped and marked (Barcia 1996) at what we called Transect 4 marsh. This record extended the documented range of mud turtle on Fire Island eastward, and confirmed a written report of a mud turtle from this area in 1993 (Burnley 1993).

In the current survey, a severe drought caused many of the wetlands on the island to remain dry for most of the 2002 season, and traps were set in pond basins with limited or no water. Although many wetland sites were searched and trapped (Tables 10, 12) only one male mud turtle was captured, on 6 June 2002 (Table 12, Appendix D) as heavy rains filled Bigfoot Pond, a temporary pond located approximately 0.75 km (0.5 mi) southeast of Bellport Bay Ditches and 0.25 km (0.2 mi) west of the washover (Figure 14). One un-marked eastern mud turtle shell was also found in the uplands near Bigfoot Pond during a visual encounter survey (Table 9). Although there were records of mud turtles to the east and west, no eastern mud turtles had previously been recorded from the Bigfoot Pond area.

Because of the limited success in finding mud turtles in 2002, presumably due to the drought, additional trapping was conducted in 2003. Frequent rain created more favorable conditions in 2003, and Bellport Bay Ditches, Bigfoot Pond, and Transect 4 Marsh were intensively trapped daily from 17 May to 5 June 2003, a time of year when mud turtles are most likely to be captured in traps (Norm Soule pers. com.). Trapping in 2003 produced 15 captures of 12 individuals as follows: Bellport Bay Ditches (4 individuals, 7 captures, CR=1.5); Bigfoot Pond (4 individuals, 4 captures, CR=2.2); and Transect 4 Marsh (4 individuals, 4 captures, CR=2.4) (Table 13, Appendix D). Two of the individuals captured in 2003 had been marked previously. One was the live individual marked in 2002 (R1) and the second, an old female with a very worn carapace captured at Transect 4 Marsh on 6/2/03, had an old mark on scute L4 (Appendix D). The only record of an animal with this scute marked is one captured as a juvenile (carapace length 53.9 mm) in the Bellport Bay ditches and marked L4R3 by Marsha Meyer in 1990. Although there are some problems in matching up these two captures, e.g. the turtle was sexed a male (not female) in 1990 (while actually still a juvenile) and in 2003 there was no evidence of a mark in R3, this happens often with animals marked and sexed as juveniles and recaptured many years later. Marks can be obscured by regrowth over time. Because there are no other animals previously notched on L4, this appears to be a re-capture. Thus, this animal has grown from 53.9 to 97.2 mm CL in 13 years, and has moved ca. 2160 meters, straight-line distance.

Comparing the abundance from 1988-90 to 2002-2003 is difficult, given the differences in conditions, sites sampled, and different methods used. The number of mud turtle captures (and unique individuals) in the Bellport Bay Ditches in 1988 was 15 (12), much greater than the four (4) in 2003. However, when based only on trapping, there were six captures and four individuals in 1988 and four captures and four individuals in 2003, with capture rates nearly identical: 1.6 captures/100 trapnight in 1988 and 1.5 in 2003. Clearly, capture rates of traps were comparable, but most of the captures in 1988 (9 of 15) were by hand during searches. In contrast, there were no hand captures in the 2002-2003 survey. The lack of any hand captures in 2002, despite 77.7 wetland search hours (Table 10) is likely due to drought-related inactivity whereas the lack of hand captures in 2003 appears to be due to a lack of search effort. Thus, there is no way to know how many additional individuals and captures might have been added to those caught in traps in the Bellport Bay Ditches.

Individuals captured in Transect 4 Marsh and Bigfoot Pond in 2003 show that mud turtles are more widespread in OPWA than was known in 1988-90, and in 2003 these sites were comparable to or greater than the Bellport Bay Ditches in numbers of mud turtles (Table 13, Appendix D). Since these sites were not sampled in 1988-90, there is no way to know how many mud turtles occurred in these wetlands then. Thus, although some of the present data (i.e. trapping in Bellport Bay ditches) suggest that mud turtle abundance is comparable between 1988 and the present survey, differences in methods and sampling locations preclude a more definitive comparison.

In terms of size and age structure, the size distribution of mud turtles found on Fire Island in 2002-2003 (Figure 16) shows a diversity of sizes, including some recent young. Mean carapace length (CL) of individuals captured in 1988-90 (75.95 mm) is not significantly different from those captured in 2003 (74.97 mm; $t=0.125$, $p=0.90$) and the proportion of juveniles in 2003 (42%) did not differ significantly from 1988-90 (36%) (Fisher's exact test $p=1.000$). These metrics suggest that there have been no changes in the structure of the mud turtle population.

To better understand habitat use and movements by FIIS mud turtles, radio transmitters were attached to seven eastern mud turtles, captured in Bigfoot Pond (3 turtles), Transect 4 Marsh (3 turtles), and Bellport Bay Ditches (1 turtle). Two did not provide any movement data, because the signal from one was never re-located and the radio fell off the other. Of the five that did provide movement data, three were monitored daily from May 20 or 21st until June 3, 2003. Beyond 6/3/03, two of these three, plus two additional turtles, were checked every 3-4 weeks, through 8/16/03 (Table 18).

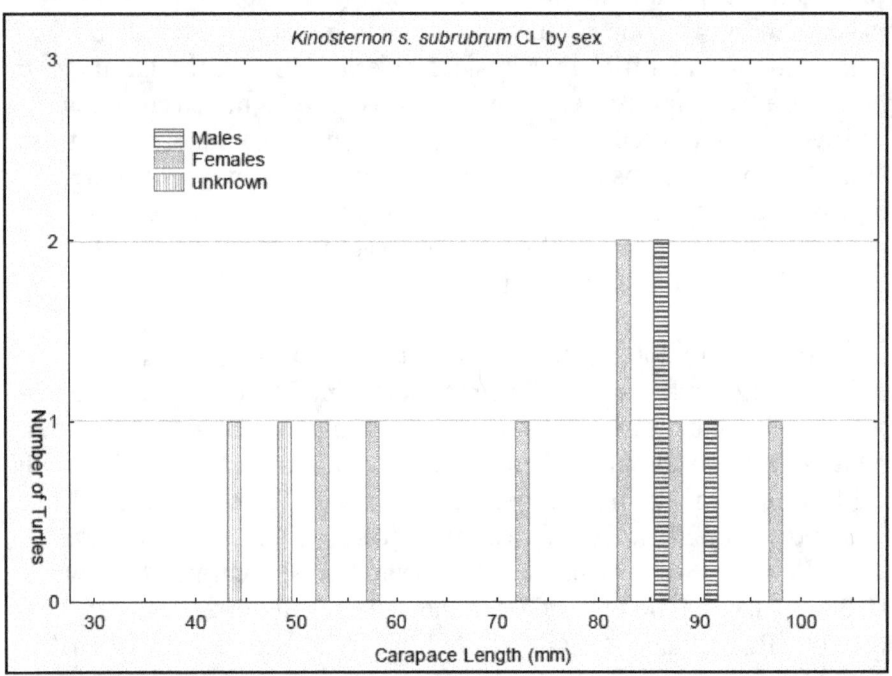

Figure 16. Frequency distribution of eastern mud turtles (*Kinosternon s. subrubrum*) by size and sex on FIIS, 2002 and 2003.

Table 18. Summary of movement data for eastern mud turtles radio-tracked on FIIS in 2003.

ID	Sex	Initial Capture Location	First Date	Last Date	Duration (days)	Total Points	Mean Daily Distance	Cumulative Distance	Net Distance
R3	F	bigfoot pond	5/21/03	6/3/03	13	13	4.52	58.82	37.48
R1,2	M	bigfoot pond	5/21/03	8/16/03	87	17	2.02	176.10	7.00
R2	M	transect 4 marsh	5/20/03	6/22/03	33	15	3.81	125.75	5.39
L1	F	bigfoot pond	6/3/03	8/16/03	74	4	5.06	374.67	200.42
R8	F	BB OI ditches	6/3/03	8/16/03	74	3	0.74	54.85	25.71
R2,8	F	transect 4 marsh	6/3/03	6/3/03	0	1	no data	no data	no data
L4	F	transect 4 marsh	6/3/03	6/3/03	0	1	no data	no data	no data

The two turtles monitored in Bigfoot Pond (Figure 17) remained in and around the pond basin. One of these, female (R3), moved upslope from 29 May to 3 June 2003 onto dry land into dense grasses at the eastern end of the pond. Eastern mud turtles nest on open ground, in sandy soil and dense vegetation not far from water. Female (R3) may have been moving towards a nesting site, but because most mud turtle nesting on Long Island occurs in June and July (Nichols 1947), the tracking data for this individual do not cover this period. Eastern mud turtles will also leave the water in the late spring or early summer and remain on land until the following spring, aestivating and hibernating in upland habitat. During dry periods, mud turtles will travel 1-600m on land, generally short distances at a time, seeking out wet areas, or they will burrow into the mud and aestivate (Ernst et al. 1994). Mud turtle L1 moved from Bigfoot Pond to the Bellport Bay ditches, and then back and forth to a point in-between, traveling about 200m net and 375m cumulative distance (Table 18, Figure 18). Mud turtles monitored in Transect 4 Marsh (Figure 19) remained in the marsh and traveled throughout it as the water level increased and connected several small ponds into one large wetland up to 45 cm deep. One mud turtle (R8) in the Bellport Bay Ditches was tracked to a small, shallow pond approximately 50 m southeast of the ditches (Figure 20).

Movement by eastern mud turtles, particularly in upland habitats is generally short distance/slow (<2 m/day), with occasional longer distance/faster movements (10 m/day), with an overall mean of 3.6 m/day (Bennett et al. 1970). In nesting female mud turtles, terrestrial movement is characterized by periods of inactivity and then longer distance movements following rainstorms (Burke et al. 1994), which is consistent with the pattern found by Bennett et al. (1970). Although limited by sample size and duration, our data suggest that FIIS mud turtles move at similar daily rates (Table 18) and moved distances similar to those recorded in other mud turtle populations over comparable time periods. For example, the mean net distance moved by the five FIIS mud turtles (55.2 m) is similar to the 44.65 m mean net distance moved by individuals followed for less than 100 days in Oklahoma (Mahmoud 1969). Bennett et al. (1970) found a significant positive correlation between net distance moved by individuals and duration of tracking, but there was no such relationship in our data (Pearson's $r=0.24$, $p=0.70$, n=5). These short term movements within and between wetlands, plus the long term movement of L4 from Bellport Bay Ditches in 1990 to Transect 4 marshes in 2003 indicate that individual mud turtles in the OPWA engage in movements typical of the species and utilize a range of wetlands, both freshwater and salt, and suggest that an individual's range over a lifetime may be much larger than short term ranges.

Previously well documented in the Bellport Bay Ditches, the eastern mud turtle was considered rare in the park. Our results show this species is slightly more widespread than previously realized, and occurs throughout the eastern half of OPWA. The western half of OPWA contains similar habitat and may also support mud turtles, but has never been sampled for them because of the logistical challenges. Although it is rare here, the FIIS population of mud turtles appears to be stable, and is one of only a small number of populations still remaining in New York State. FIIS is thus an important site for eastern mud turtle, particularly since it is mostly protected from the various stressors negatively impacting this species elsewhere on Long Island. Given its NY State *Endangered* status and the significance of FIIS for this species, more detailed surveys throughout the entire OPWA are recommended to better estimate overall distribution and population size and structure.

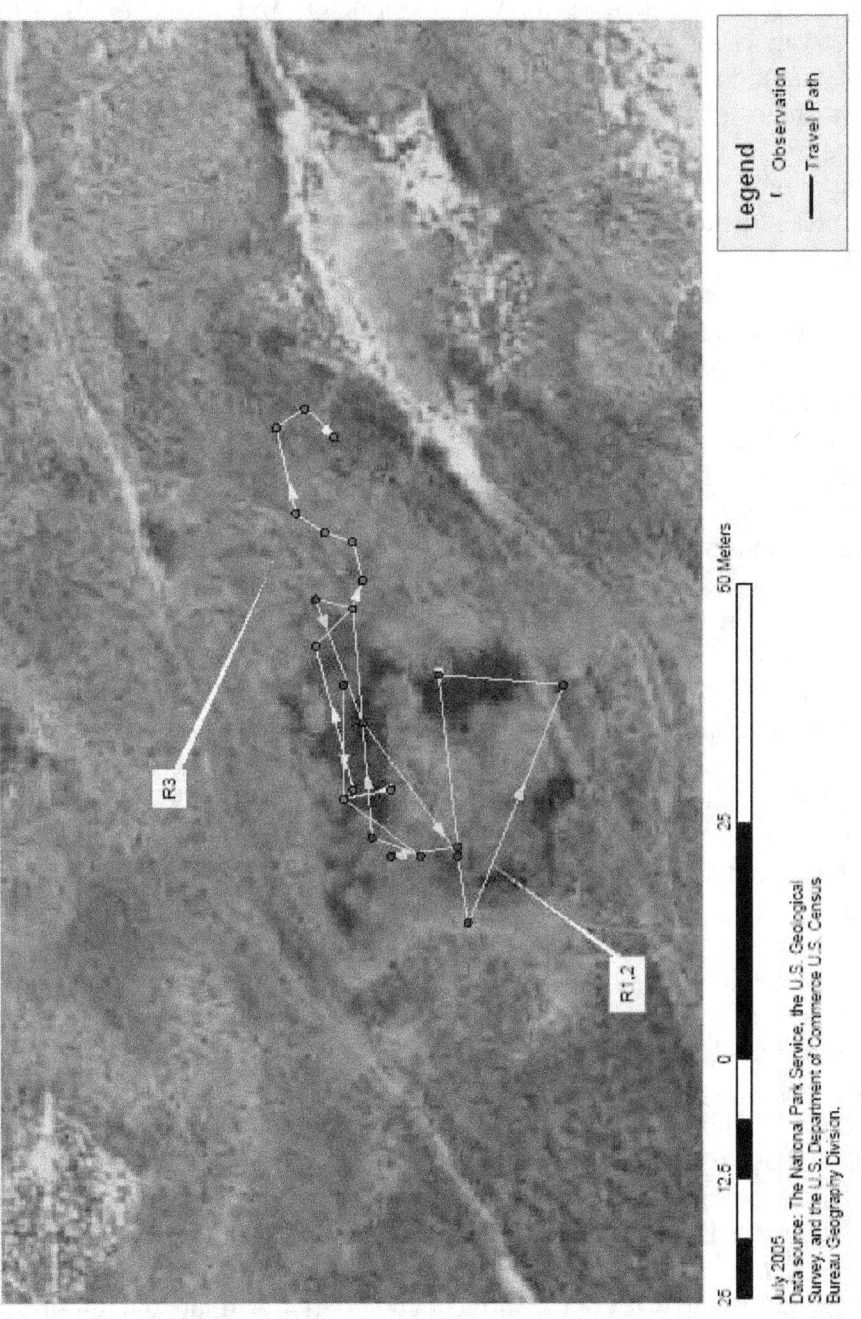

Figure 17. Movement of eastern mud turtles R1-2 and R3 in Bigfoot pond in 2003.

68

Fire Island National Seashore
Herpetological Survey

Eastern mud turtle *(Kinosternon s. subrubrum)*
L1 Movements

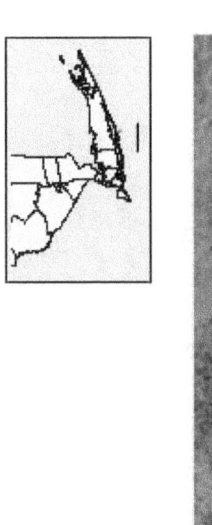

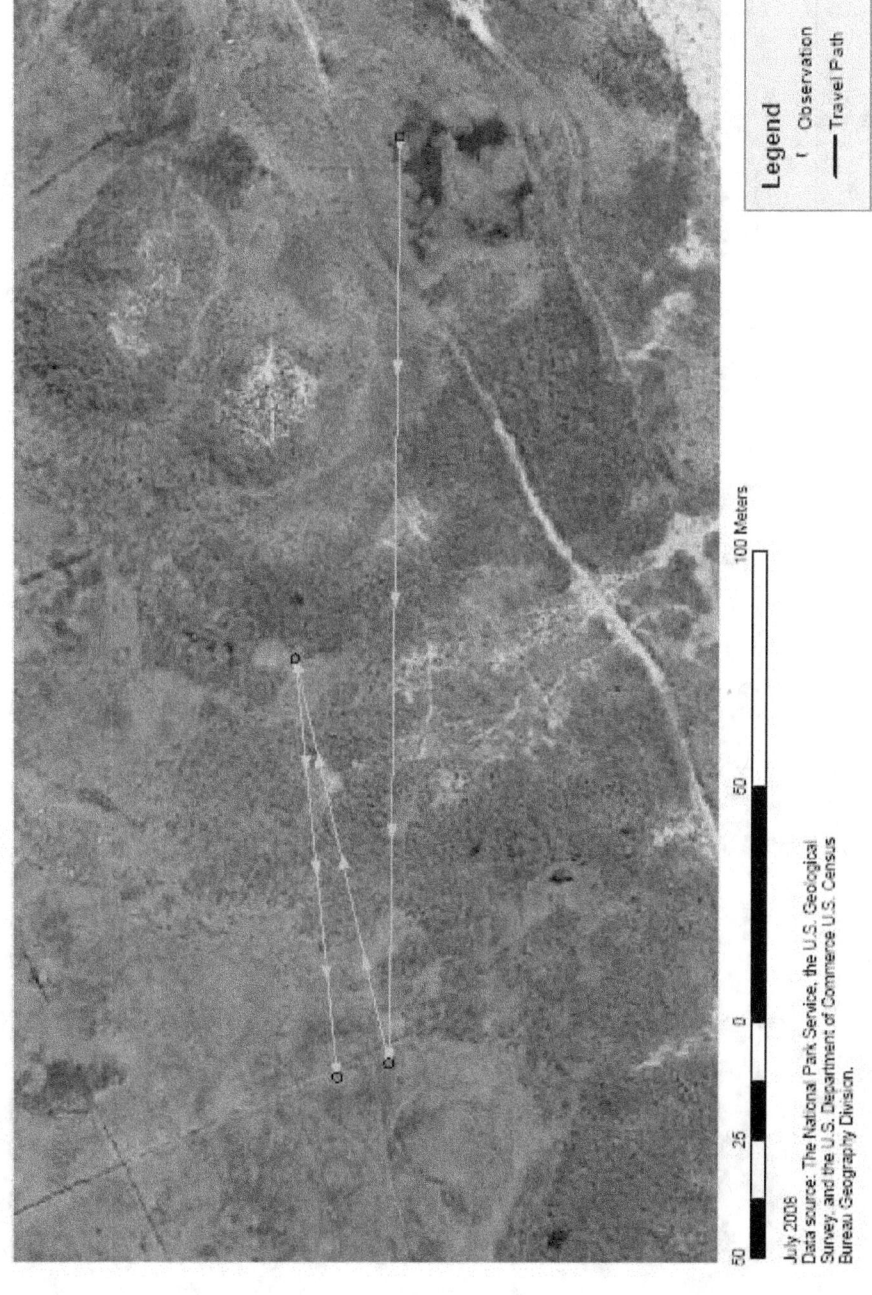

July 2008
Data source: The National Park Service, the U.S. Geological
Survey, and the U.S. Department of Commerce U.S. Census
Bureau Geography Division.

50   25   0   50   100 Meters

Legend
ꞁ   Observation
—   Travel Path

Figure 18. Movements of eastern mud turtle L1 from Bigfoot Pond between 3 June and 16 August 2003.

Fire Island National Seashore
Herpetological Survey

Eastern mud turtle (*Kinosternon s. subrubrum*)
R2 and R2,8 Movements

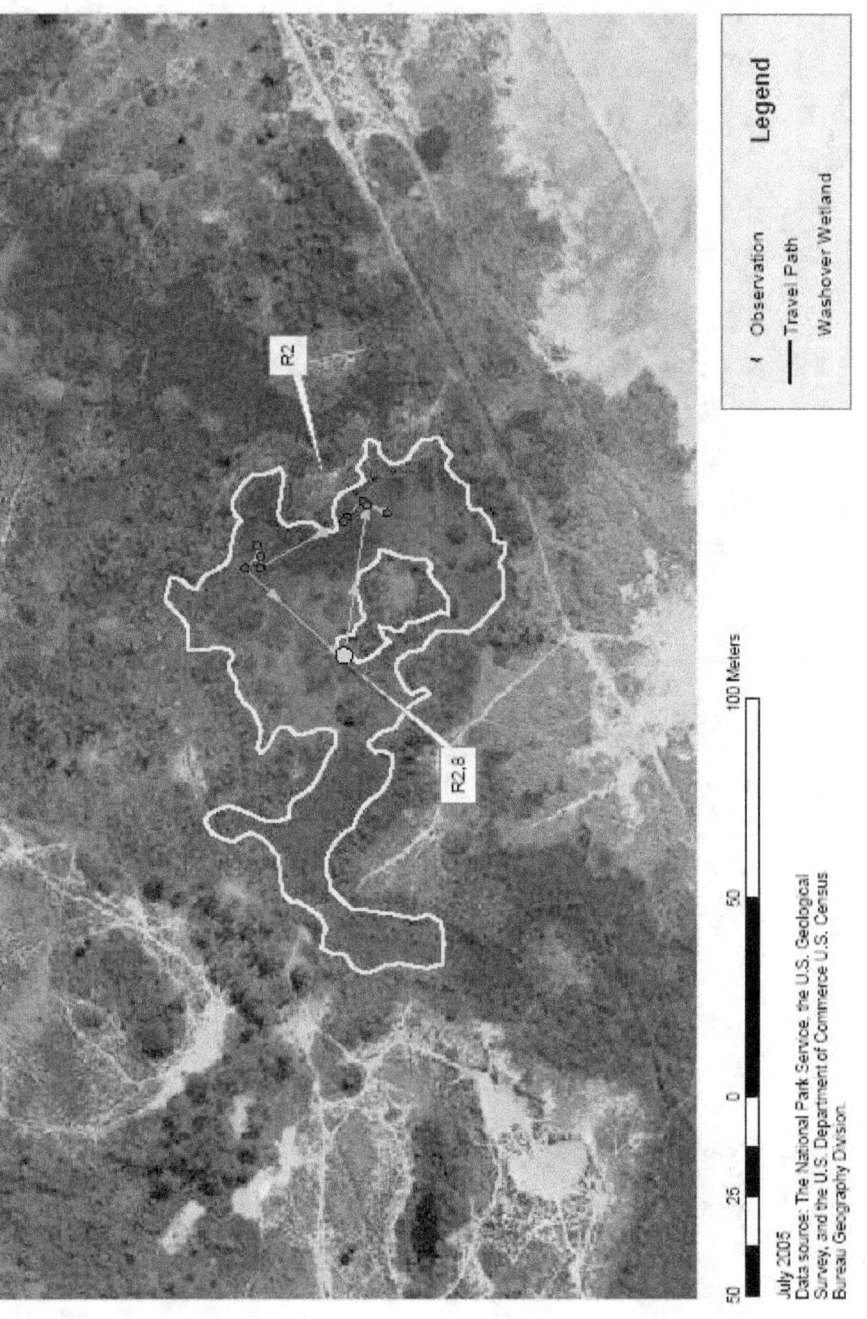

July 2005
Data source: The National Park Service, the U.S. Geological
Survey, and the U.S. Department of Commerce U.S. Census
Bureau Geography Division.

Legend

↑ Observation

—— Travel Path

Washover Wetland

Figure 19. Movements of eastern mud turtle R2 in Transect 4 Marsh in between 20 May to 6 June 2003.

Fire Island National Seashore
Herpetological Survey

Eastern mud turtle *(Kinosternon s. subrubrum)*
R1-3, R2-3, R8, and L2 capture locations in Bellport Bay Ditches

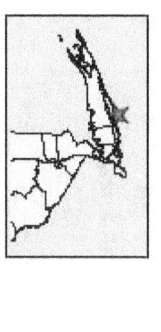

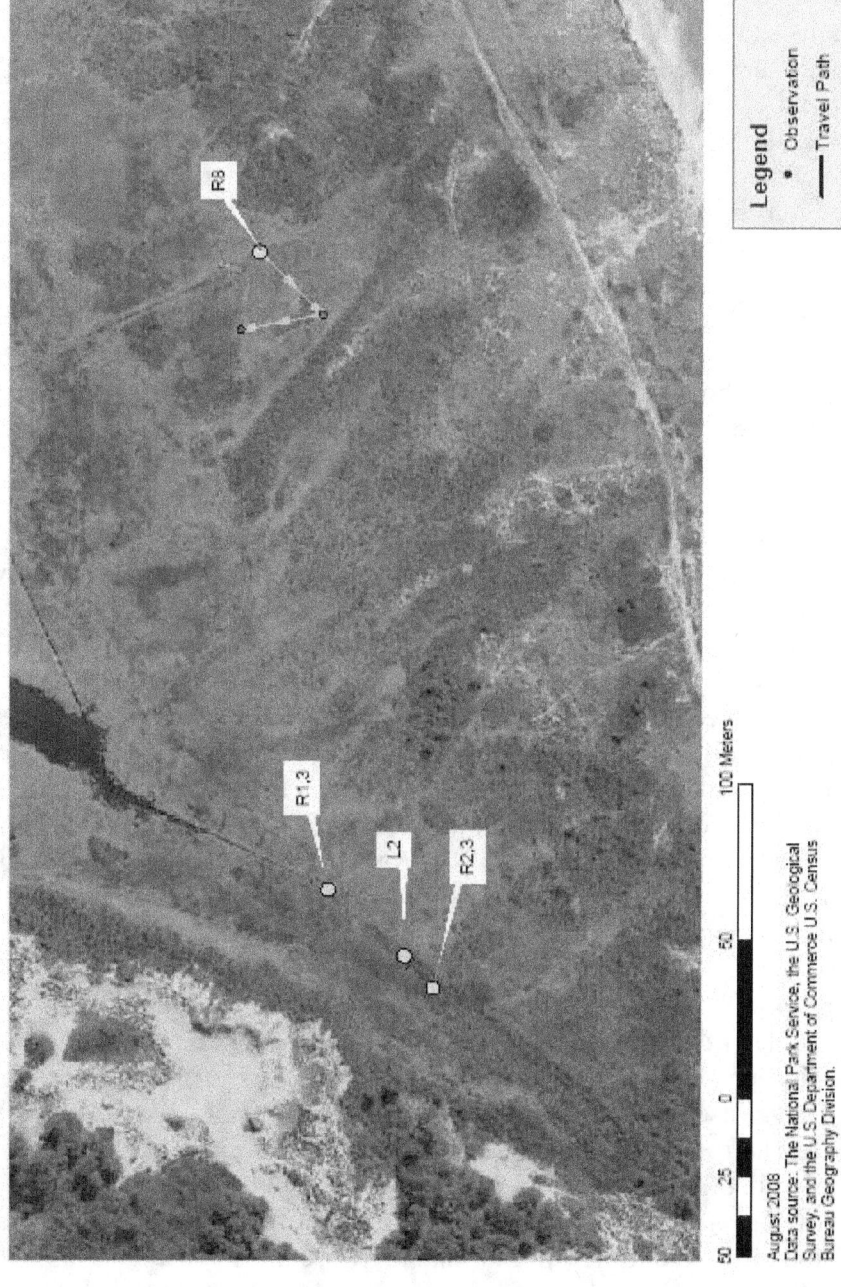

Figure 20. Capture locations of eastern mud turtle R1-3, L2, and R2-3 and movements of R8 in Bellport Bay Ditches.

Spotted Turtle (*Clemmys guttata*)

A small semi-aquatic turtle with distinct yellow spots on a black carapace, the spotted turtle occurs along the Atlantic coastal plain, from Maine to Florida, including lower elevation areas of southern New England (Klemens 1993), and westward into Ohio, Indiana, Illinois, Michigan, and southeastern Canada (Ernst et al. 1994). In New York, spotted turtles occur in western New York, south of Lake Erie, in the Hudson River Valley, and on Long Island and Staten Island (Gibbs et al. 2007). Although spotted turtles are widespread, they primarily occur in a broad range of shallow habitats, both freshwater and slightly saline and are considered semi-aquatic, because they may spend a lot of time on land when temporary wetlands dry (Ernst et al. 1994). Historically, spotted turtles were common and widespread in the New York City area, occurring in ponds, streams and salt marshes (Smith 1899, Murphy 1916, Noble 1927). Nichols (1914) noted that spotted turtles were abundant in the salt meadow creeks of Mastic, opposite Fire Island. By the mid-20th century, the negative impacts of urbanization on them were becoming apparent (Kieran 1959). This decline was due to the loss of preferred wetland habitats to urbanization (Schlauch 1976), exacerbated by their complex patterns of seasonal habitat shifts and large home ranges, which make them very susceptible to the negative impacts of habitat fragmentation (Klemens 1993). In addition, given the extensive use of DDT on the south shore of Long Island (Jankowski 2004), and its negative effects on reptiles via direct mortality and endocrine disruption (Guillette 2000), it is likely that pesticides have also contributed to the spotted turtle's decline on Long Island. They are currently listed by New York State as a species of *Special Concern*. They are rare and very limited in NYC, but a bit more common eastward on Long Island, with one site in Nassau County and several in Suffolk County (Breisch and Ozard in prep).

In the course of this survey, there were 11 spotted turtle captures (Table 2) involving eight individuals. In 2002, seven adults were captured in the Watch Hill area. Three were each re-captured once, for a total of 10 captures (Table 4). Of these seven individuals, two were captured in the marsh under the Watch Hill boardwalk and five were captured at Watch Hill Pond 37 (Appendix D). None were previously marked. These two "sites" are in close proximity and hydrologically connected. This entire area was mapped as a single extensive wetland by Caldecutt (1997) and all of these individuals are part of a single population. Prior surveys have also found a small population of spotted turtles at Watch Hill (Caldecutt 1997; Barcia 1996; Putnam 1999) and this area appears to be the most significant on Fire Island for this species. However, a dead specimen found in the OPWA (Northup 1986) and an individual captured (but not marked) on 18 May 2003 from Sailor's Haven near the east end of Sunken Forest (Steve Finn pers. comm.) indicate that spotted turtles have a wider range on the island.

With no data prior to the 1980's, it is impossible to discuss long term trends. Shorter term trends, over the past couple of decades, suggest the spotted turtle remains uncommon in the park and is slightly more widespread than originally known. The size/age structure, with only adults found (Appendix D), suggests that spotted turtles are not reproducing successfully very often. At Cape Cod National Seashore, 9.8% of spotted turtles recorded were juveniles, and the proportion of juveniles recorded in other populations ranged from 4,2% to 23.3% (Cook et al. 2007). A sample size of seven is too small to say much about size, structure, reproductive success, movements, or habitat utilization of spotted turtles on Fire Island. More intensive and sustained sampling in Sunken Forest, Sailor's Haven, Watch Hill, and similar wetlands in the park is recommended to better understand its status and long-term prospects. In addition, searches in bayside ditches are recommended as spotted turtles are able to tolerate slightly brackish conditions and will utilize the inland areas of mosquito ditches (Ernst et al. 1994; J. Behler pers. obs.).

Eastern Box Turtle (*Terrapene carolina carolina*)

Eastern box turtles occur from Georgia and northern Alabama and Mississippi northward into southern Illinois and eastward (Conant and Collins 1998). In the northeast and New England, box turtles are largely restricted to the coastal plain and major river valleys (Klemens 1993). The eastern box turtle is a terrestrial species that typically occurs in areas that are a mix of woodland and open habitat. The habitat diversity provides the ability to shift habitats seasonally in response to changes in temperature and humidity (Reagan 1974), and, as with all turtles, well drained open habitats provide nesting sites. This long-lived species is known to live more than a century (Oliver 1955; Graham and Hutchison 1969). Eastern box turtles are frequently found foraging following spring and summer rains, and they will feed on slugs, fruits, vegetation and carrion.

Historically, box turtles were widespread in the New York metropolitan area and considered abundant on Long Island (Smith 1899; Engelhardt 1913; Murphy 1916; Noble 1927). However, as urbanization progressed they began to decline. Citing automobiles as a cause, Kieran (1959) noted the decline of box turtles in all boroughs of NYC, except Staten Island. The terrestrial nature of box turtles results in their being more widely dispersed across the landscape than aquatic amphibians and reptiles. Box turtles often engage in seasonal movements for nesting, hibernation, or feeding, and some individuals are transients that do not establish home ranges (Dodd 2001). All this movement across the landscape places box turtles at relatively greater risk of becoming road kill or being collected for a pet in urban areas, which, in conjunction with their late maturity and low rate of reproduction, make their populations unable to sustain the heavy adult mortality that typically occurs in urban areas. Thus, box turtle populations do not fare well on the highly fragmented landscapes found in urban/suburban areas (Schlauch 1976, Mitchell and Klemens 2000) and are declining in many parts of their range (Dodd 2001). Box turtles are a species of *Special Concern* in New York State and although there are still many, widespread records from Long Island (Breisch and Ozard, in prep) they are found primarily in parks and habitat remnants (Klemens 1993). Moreover, box turtles are frequently moved around and released by people, and because they are long lived, many of these recent records, especially on western Long Island, do not necessarily mean that a viable population is still present.

Box turtles were among the most common turtles, with a total of 24 individuals recorded in this survey. They were also the second most widespread species, recorded from 11 sites (FO=27%) and four of six tracts (Tables 2, 3, 4, 5). Of these 24 individuals, six were shells of dead individuals. Of the remaining 18 live captures, 17 were marked and measured (Figure 21). Of these 17 individuals, 14 were adults (Appendix D). Geographically, the majority of individuals (15/24) were recorded from the Sunken Forest uplands and ponds, but box turtles were recorded from throughout the park, including two individuals captured in the communities of Point O'Woods and Ocean Beach (Table 4). Eastern box turtles were previously known to occur in Ocean Beach, and local citizens have "monitored" them for years (Steve Finn pers. comm.).

Prior records of eastern box turtles on FIIS (Smith 1962; Northup 1986; Barcia 1996; Caldecutt 1997; Putnam 1999) suggest this species was common. Searches in 2002 found this to still be the case, with the majority of eastern box turtles occupying the Sunken Forest area. Sunken Forest provides the best available habitat on Fire Island for this species with large, contiguous woodlands and numerous temporary freshwater ponds. Because young box turtles are more vulnerable to predation and tend to be less conspicuous, most studies of box turtle populations record primarily adults (Dodd 2001). The proportion of adults recorded on FIIS (82%) is consistent with this, and very similar to the 80.5% found on the William Floyd Estate in Mastic during the early 20th century (Nichols 1939). That the current population in FIIS has a similar proportion of juveniles as was found decades ago on a site known for its robust population of box turtles, suggests a healthy population structure with successful recruitment occurring.

Although box turtles appear to be absent from barrier islands in the Southeast United States (Gibbons and Coker 1978), they occur on barrier islands and spits in the Northeast (Mitchell and Anderson 1994; Cook in prep,). Smith (1962) seemed puzzled by the presence of box turtles on Fire Island and Jones Island (to the west), but there are many observations of Long Island box turtles swimming in salt water bays and creeks (Cook 1996) and no reason to think box turtles did not colonize Fire Island naturally. However, it is also likely that some box turtles have been rescued while crossing roads and eventually released here. Given the decline that box turtles are experiencing both locally and range-wide, primarily from the cumulative impacts of urbanization and habitat fragmentation (Dodd 2001), FIIS, with its largely roadless and heterogeneous landscape, provides an important refuge for this species.

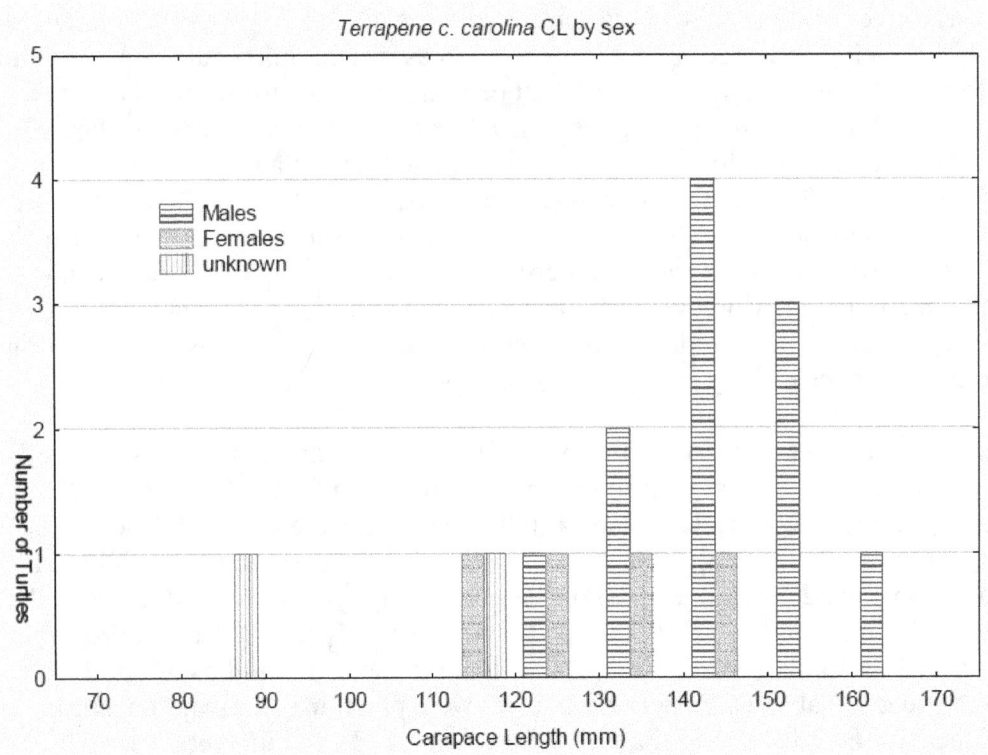

Figure 21. Frequency distribution of eastern box turtles (*Terrapene c. carolina*) by size and sex on FIIS, 2002.

Painted Turtle (*Chrysemys picta*)

The painted turtle is the only North American turtle that ranges across the continent, from southern Canada down through the Pacific northwest, midwest, and the northeast coast to Louisiana, Georgia, and the Carolinas (Ernst et al. 1994). There are four subspecies, with standard English names that describe each subspecies' distribution. In the Northeast and New England, including the New York City - Long Island region, the Eastern painted turtle (*C. p. picta*) and the Midland painted turtle (*C. p. marginata*) intergrade, forming a hybrid swarm (Pough and Pough 1968). Whereas the eastern painted turtle has an unmarked yellow plastron and the seams of the central and lateral carapace scutes are aligned and the midland painted turtle has a variable dark marking on the plastron and alternating seams on the carapacial scutes (Ernst et al. 1994), Long Island painted turtles are intermediate in these characters and are highly variable both within and among populations (Pough and Pough 1968).

In addition to a wide geographic distribution, painted turtles are widespread ecologically, occurring in a broad range of freshwater habitats, including vernal ponds. However, they prefer permanent, shallow standing or slow-moving water bodies with soft bottoms and an abundance of aquatic vegetation (Ernst et al. 1994; Cook et al. 2007; Gibbs et al. 2007). Because of their abundance and habit of basking on rocks, logs, and clumps of vegetation, painted turtles are the region's most familiar and conspicuous turtle (Klemens 1993). Painted turtles are highly aquatic, feeding and hibernating in ponds. However, they lay their eggs on land and, as with all aquatic turtles, must leave the relative safety of the wetland and travel overland to patches of open habitat with well drained soils to nest.

Historically, painted turtles were considered widespread and very abundant in the New York City-Long Island region (Engelhardt 1913; Murphy 1916; Noble 1927). Because permanent water bodies are more likely to survive urbanization and have increased in some instances through the damming of streams, painted turtles in the NYC region survived 20th century urbanization (Mathewson 1955; Kieran 1959; Schlauch 1978) and remain widespread today. They occur in most any natural area with a permanent pond or lake (Breisch and Ozard in prep).

In spite of their widespread occurrence on Long Island, including the Patchogue River across from Fire Island (R. Stavdal pers. comm.), and the occurrence of painted turtles on other barrier spits and islands, such as Sandy Hook, NJ (Cook in prep.) and Assateague Island (Mitchell and Anderson 1994), there is no evidence that painted turtles ever occurred on Fire Island. McCormick (1975) lists the painted turtle as occurring on Fire Island, but provides no basis for its inclusion. Northup (1986) did not observe any painted turtles during surveys from fall 1984 through fall 1985, nor were any observed in surveys by Caldecutt (1997), Putnam (1999), nor in the current survey. Because permanent pond habitat is so limited on FIIS, we considered that the painted turtle, if present, would most likely occur in Kismet Pond. Accordingly, this site was sampled intensively with turtle traps, drift fences, and visual surveys (Table 1) without any being recorded. In addition, none of the NPS staff contacted who worked, and in some cases lived on Fire Island during the 1970's, 1980's and 1990's ever observed any on island (S. Finn pers. comm.; ML. Lamont pers. comm.; R. Rozsa pers. comm.; R. Stavdal pers. comm.).

Given how conspicuous and pollution/disturbance tolerant painted turtles are (Klemens 1993; Gibbs et al. 2007) it is unlikely that painted turtles have eluded detection all these years or have been extirpated. A more plausible explanation is that they do not occur on Fire Island and never did. Although painted turtles tolerate slightly brackish water, they are not as tolerant of it as the other turtle species found on FIIS (Ernst et al. 1994). In addition, permanent freshwater habitat on FIIS is very limited and located far from the original point of contact with the mainland, where overland colonization would have occurred. These two factors would have limited the likelihood of successful natural colonization of FIIS by painted turtles. For all these reasons, painted turtles are not considered part of the historic or present-day herpetofauna of FIIS.

Northern Diamond-backed Terrapin (*Malaclemys terrapin terrapin*)

The northern diamond-backed terrapin is a sub-species of the diamond-backed terrapin, a species that ranges along the coast from Texas to Cape Cod, Massachusetts. Northern diamond-backed terrapins range from Cape Hatteras, North Carolina to Cape Cod (Conant and Collins 1998). In New York, diamond-backed terrapins occur primarily along the coast of Long Island, both north and south shore (Morreale 1992). Terrapins are unique in that they are the only species of turtle restricted to estuaries (Morreale 1992), and they are typically found wherever extensive salt marsh habitat has developed, such as behind barrier beaches and within deep embayments. Although they spend most of their time in salt marshes, where they forage primarily on mollusks and crabs, female diamond-backed terrapins must emerge onto land to lay eggs, nesting in dunes, along roads and trails, and other open situations, often several hundred meters from water (Brennessel 2006). On western Long Island, terrapins nest from the first week of June through the third week of July (Cook 1989; Feinberg and Burke 2003).

Historically, diamond-backed terrapins were widespread and abundant in the New York metropolitan area. However, they were highly valued as a delicacy (Smith 1899) and by the late 19th-early 20th century they had declined due to overharvesting (Engelhardt 1913; Murphy 1916). Terrapins remained rare to uncommon in the region during the first half of the 20th century, but appeared to be rebounding by the second half (Yeaton 1972; Morreale 1992). By the late 20th century, diamond-backed terrapins had recovered in many areas, including Long Island, although it was noted that the continuation of this recovery was threatened by renewed loss of habitat, commercial take, drowning in crab pots, and roadkill (Cook1989; Wood and Herlands 1997). In addition, where raccoons are present, particularly as subsidized predators, nest predation can be a significant problem. At Jamaica Bay Wildlife Refuge on western Long Island, where there was a large increase in the raccoon population, nest depredation by raccoons went from none in the early 1980's (Cook 1989) to 92.2% by the late 1990's (Feinberg and Burke 2003).

In the present survey, northern diamond-backed terrapin was among the most abundant turtles on FIIS, with a total of 25 records. Recorded from 7 sites (FO=17.1%), they were moderately widespread by this measure, but all records were in the Watch Hill-OPWA tracts (Tables 2,3,4,5). Of the 25 records, there were two live adults and one live hatchling (Appendix D), nine nests, eight adult shells, three juvenile shells, and two dead hatchlings. An adult female was observed on 5 June 2002 nesting in an open, sandy area of the old Burma Road (OPWA), approximately 1 km west of the Smith Point Visitor Center. The nest was marked and monitored for the next three months and since no hatchlings had yet emerged, the nest was excavated on 3 September. A total of 13 undeveloped eggs were found.

Although we have no real knowledge of trends in the terrapin population on FIIS during the early and mid 20th century, the collective impression from several reports (Northup 1986; Meyer 1988; Barcia 1996; Caldecutt 1997; Putnam 1999) is that in the 1990's they were fairly common. Since diamond-backed terrapins spend most of their time in the bay and associated estuaries, and searches during this survey were concentrated in freshwater wetlands and uplands (with some trapping in ditches), our results likely under-represent the local population. Further trapping for adults near the ditches and in the bay, and searches for nesting females in the open sandy areas of the wilderness area and islands in the bay would help to better understand the size, structure, nesting success, habitat utilization, and distribution of the northern diamond-backed terrapin on FIIS. However, despite these data limitations, our results suggest that terrapins continue to be fairly common on Fire Island and that the island, especially the Watch Hill-OPWA tracts, continues to be an important area for this species.

Northern Black Racer (*Coluber constrictor constrictor*)

The northern black racer is subspecies of the eastern racer, which is widespread throughout most of the United States, except for the desert southwest (Ernst and Ernst 2003). The northern black racer occurs from the southern Appalachian Mountains northward, extending to the coastal plain in the mid-Atlantic states and into southern New York and southern New England (Conant and Collins 1998). The black racer is widespread in New Jersey, southern New York and New England, but occurs primarily at relatively low elevations along the coast and in river valleys (Trapido 1937; Klemens, 1993; Gibbs et al. 2007). It is found in open, dry woodlands, fields, grasslands, along the borders of wetlands, and on barrier islands (Ernst and Ernst 2003). Large sheets of corrugated sheet metal and plywood are a favorite cover type of this species, along with other debris at the edge of woodlands (Klemens 1993). Juvenile northern black racers have distinct gray/brown or reddish/brown patterning down their bluish/gray back that will disappear as they mature. Adults are satiny black in color with a white throat patch and can reach five to six feet in length (Conant and Collins 1998). An opportunistic feeder, the racer diet includes a variety of animals such as shrews, voles, birds, small turtles, lizards, anurans, salamanders, and snakes (including hog-nosed snake *Herterdon platirhinos*) (Ernst and Ernst 2003).

Historically, the black racer was common and widespread in the New York City region (Noble 1927) and on Long Island it was especially common along the sandy south shore (Engelhardt et al. 1915). Black racers occur primarily in landscapes with open habitats and are a large, conspicuously active species with a large home range (Ernst and Ernst 2003; Kjoss and Litvaitis, 2001). As the flat, open habitats in the region were easily developed, the behaviors and large home range of black racers lead to greater mortality in landscapes fragmented by urbanization (Schlauch 1976; Gibbs et al. 2007). Intentional killing by humans was also a factor (Mathewson 1955). By mid-20th century, black racers had declined through much of western Long Island (Kieran 1959) and its current distribution on Long Island is primarily in wilder sections of Suffolk County (Breisch and Ozard in prep). On Fire Island, Murphy (1950) noted their presence, but saw only one and Northup (1986) considered them fairly common and widespread.

In 2002, the northern black racer was among the most common and widely distributed species recorded. Based on a total of 28 records (12 captures, 9 observations, 5 nests, and 2 shed skins), it was the most common (RA=82.4%) and widespread (FO=22%) snake species (Tables 2, 3). The size distribution of animals captured, nine adults and three juveniles (Appendix E), plus five nests, indicates there is active breeding and recruitment. An old hatched out nest was found under a board in the open, sandy OPWA Washover area on 8 April 2002. A new nest was found under the same board on 6 August 2002, and when inspected on 3 September 2002, most of the eggs had hatched out. Although limited, both "historic" and more recent information (Northup 1986; Caldecutt 1997; Putnam 1999) including this survey, indicate that black racers are and continue to be widespread and common on Fire Island. The island's relatively roadless and unfragmented nature, the patchiness of its extensive open, early successional-state vegetation, and the protection conferred on wildlife by the National Park Service make Fire Island an ideal landscape for black racers. Given their historic declines throughout most of the region and concerns that continued fragmentation and ecological succession will cause further declines (Gibbs et al. 2007), Fire Island is a regionally important site for maintaining viable populations of black racers.

Eastern Hog-nosed Snake (*Heterdon platirhinos*)

The eastern hog-nosed snake, a species of *Special Concern* in New York, occurs throughout most of the central and eastern U.S. and into southern Canada (Ernst and Ernst 2003). In the northeast, hog-nosed snakes are limited to southern New York and southern New England, and much of their occurrence in this region is linked to the presence of sandy habitat: it prefers sandy, well-drained soils in woodlands, fields, and on barrier beaches (Klemens 1993; Ernst and Ernst 2003; Gibbs et al. 2007). Historically, hog-nosed snakes were widespread and common in the NYC metropolitan region (Ditmars 1896; Noble 1927) and were considered particularly abundant along the south shore of Long Island (Engelhardt et al. 1915). Smith (1963) details their abundance on the barrier beaches of Long Island from Coney Island eastward to Fire Island, and Engelhardt et al. (1915) described an encounter with campers who had collected a barrel full of hog-nosed snakes in 1908 at Rockaway Beach in Queens. Yeaton (1974) also recounted stories of "barrels of adders being collected under Fire Island boardwalks in the olden days"

Hog-nosed snakes have a number of specialized attributes that make them both readily identifiable and especially vulnerable. Their upturned rostral scale at the tip of the snout and their bizarre defensive behaviors are unique among local species. When threatened, the eastern hog-nosed snake will puff up and hiss loudly, flatten the head into a "hood", and sometimes attempt to strike with a closed mouth. The snake will regurgitate its last meal, turn on its back with its mouth open, and feign death. Although harmless to humans, this behavior often leads people to kill hog-nosed snakes, thinking they are a threat. In addition, hog-nosed snakes feed almost exclusively on toads and their distribution and abundance is greatly influenced by variation in toad abundance. Consequently, hog-nosed snakes do not survive urbanization nor co-exist with humans very well. By the 1930's they were declining on Staten Island, in part due to a decline in Fowler's toad (Leng and Davis 1930). By the 1940's they were declining throughout most of Long Island, with both Murphy (1950) and Smith (1963) attributing their decline to direct killing by humans unfamiliar with their defensive displays. Kieran (1959) also noted their decline in NYC and Schlauch (1978) considered the hog-nosed snaked extremely endangered in Nassau County. They are somewhat more common on eastern Long Island (Breisch and Ozard in prep.) but still, relatively few are recorded there (J. Feinberg, pers. comm.). Hog-nosed snakes on Fire Island apparently followed this regional decline, and prior to this survey, the last one recorded was in the 1970's, despite a number of attempts to find them (Caldecut 1997; Putnam 1999). In fact, none were recorded during this survey in 2002 and 2003, despite extensive searches island-wide, and the only evidence that hog-nosed snakes are still extant on Fire Island is a single adult found by MaryLaura Lamont at Watch Hill on May 14, 2007 (ML Lamont, pers.comm.).

The decline of hog-nosed snakes on Long Island is the result of habitat destruction and fragmentation, road-kill, indiscriminant killing, and pesticides, and these factors have also likely contributed to its decline on Fire Island. However, the relative importance of these factors probably differs between the heavily suburbanized Long Island "mainland" and the more "natural" Fire Island. Habitat loss and fragmentation and associated road kill are probably not as significant on Fire Island, nor is indiscriminant killing likely to have been as intense, given the amount of "wilderness" that historically existed on the island (Murphy 1950) and the protection conferred on park wildlife and habitats since the early 1960's. Pesticides are another matter. DDT was sprayed extensively and indiscriminately to control mosquitoes in Suffolk County wetlands and grasslands for 15 years, ending in 1966, and many marine invertebrates in Great South Bay were locally extirpated (Jankowski 2004). Although quantities are unknown, DDT was also applied to Fire Island marshes during this period (Flora et al. 1992). These applications likely affected hog-nosed snakes both directly and indirectly. In the short-term, DDT is more lethal to snakes than turtles (Stickel 1951; Hall 1980) and over time, pesticides, including DDT and its decay products and metabolites, can mimic and inhibit endocrine functions and disrupt reproduction in a number of ways that reduce reproductive success and ultimately lead to population declines (Guillette 2000). In addition, DDT has been implicated regionally in the loss of Fowler's toad populations (Lazell 1976; Cook in prep.). Thus, besides possibly affecting hog-nosed snakes via direct mortality or decreased reproductive success, it is likely that applications of DDT on FIIS have affected them by reducing they primary prey, Fowlers toad. Although Fowler's toads are currently common and may have already passed through this population "bottleneck", it appears the hog-nosed snake has yet to recover.

Currently, hog-nosed snakes are extremely rare on Fire Island although they appear to be doing much better on a far more developed and heavily visited island nearby (J. Feinberg pers. comm.). Reasons for this counter-intuitive situation are unknown but warrant a closer comparison. Whether the population of hog-nosed snakes on FIIS eventually recovers still remains to be seen. Monitoring it should be a high priority. However, hog-nosed snakes can be difficult to find, even when common, and an indirect, "incidental encounter" approach is recommended. In this approach, appropriate park employees and associates are asked to bring any hog-nosed snakes they might encounter in the course of their routine activities to the natural resources staff for examination and documentation or, if that is not possible, to photo-document and record location. Such an approach has worked successfully in other NPS sites and preserves, and costs very little to implement.

Eastern Garter Snake (*Thamnophis sirtalis sirtalis*)

The eastern is a sub-species of the common garter snake, which ranges throughout the United States, except for Texas and the southwest, and all of southern Canada (Ernst and Ernst 2003). The eastern garter snake occurs primarily east of the Mississippi River from Florida northward into New York and southern New England into Canada (Conant and Collins 1998). In New York and southern New England, garter snakes are widespread and common, both inland and along the coast, and are the most conspicuous and well known snake in this area (Klemens 1993; Gibbs et al. 2007). Garter snakes are found in a variety of habitats including meadows, marshes, woodlands, and cultivated and developed areas (Behler and King 1979). Historically they were considered the most common and widespread snake around New York City (Ditmars 1896) and on Long Island (Engelhardt 1913). By the mid-20th century garter snakes were still considered the most common local snake in New York City (Kieran 1959). Although garter snakes are relatively urban tolerant because of their generalized habits (Schlauch 1976), as urbanization has continued into the late 20th century, they have become less common and widespread. However, data from the New York State Herp Atlas (Breisch and Ozard, in prep), show they still remain the most common and widespread snake locally.

On Fire Island, the eastern garter snake was uncommon, with only five individuals found from Kismet Pond and Interior. Of these five, one was captured in a drift fence pitfall trap, two dead on the road, and two near the ranger station (Tables 15 and 16, Appendix E). With an RA among snakes of 14.7% (Table 2), it was less common than the black racer. The low FO (5%) reflects its very limited occurrence on FIIS (Table 4). Garter snakes were previously recorded in freshwater wetlands near the Lighthouse Visitor Center in Kismet Interior (Caldecutt 1997), from Saltaire (Putnam 1999), and Northup (1986) mentions undocumented observations of snakes that probably are garter snakes. Similar to the American bullfrog, the limited distribution of garter snakes on Fire Island, essentially the highly accessible Lighthouse tract, and a lack of truly "historic" records suggests a recent arrival, one perhaps aided by humans. However, the historic record is incomplete and garter snakes are known from many southern barrier islands (Gibbons and Coker 1978), so their presence on Fire Island may be natural. Thus, we consider the garter snake population on Fire Island to be an uncommon, relatively stable, naturally-occurring one, but its origins are not certain.

Literature Cited

Adams, M. J. 1999. Correlated factors in amphibian decline: exotic species and habitat change in western Washington. Journal of Wildlife Management 63:1162-1171.

Bank, M. S., J. B. Crocker, S. Davis, D. K. Brotherton, R. Cook, J. Behler, and B. Connery. 2006. Population decline of northern dusky salamanders at Acadia National Park, Maine, USA. Biological Conservation 130:230-238.

Barcia, S. 1996. Trapping for eastern mud turtle (*Kinosternon subrubrum subrubrum*) in Fire Island National Seashore. Final Report. National Park Service. Patchogue, NY.

Behler, J. L., and F. W. King. 1979. The Audubon Society Field Guide to North American Reptiles and Amphibians. Alfred A. Knopf. New York, NY.

Bennett, D. H., J. W. Gibbons, and J. C. Franson. 1970. Terrestrial activity in aquatic turtles. Ecology 51:738-740.

Bien, J. R., 1895. Suffolk County, New York. Published in New York by Julius Bien. In David Rumsey Map Collection. http://www.davidrumsey.com/detail?id=1-1-26283-1110046&name=Suffolk+County

Blaustein, A. R. 1994. Chicken little or Nero's fiddle? A perspective on declining amphibian populations. Herpetologica 50:85-97.

Blaustein, A. R., P. D. Hoffman, D. G. Hokit, J. M. Kiesecker, S. C. Walls, and J. B. Hays. 1994. UV repair and resistance to solar UV-B in amphibian eggs: a link to population declines? Proceedings of the National Academy of Sciences. 91:1791-1795.

Breden, F. 1988. The natural history and ecology of Fowler's toad, *Bufo woodhousei fowleri* (Amphibia: Bufonidae) in the Indiana Dunes National Lakeshore. Fieldiana Zoology 49:1-16.

Brennessel, B. 2006. Diamonds in the marsh: a natural history of the diamondback terrapin. University Press of New England. Lebanon, NH.

Breisch, A. R. and J. W. Ozard. in prep. The New York State Amphibian and Reptile Atlas 1990-1999. New York State Department of Environmental Conservation.

Burke, V. J., J. W. Gibbons, and J. L. Greene. 1994. Prolonged nesting forays by common mud turtles (*Kinosternon subrubrum*). American Midland Naturalist 131:190-195.

Burnley, J. M. 1993. Letter to Norman Soule regarding mud turtle observation on Fire Island in 1993. National Park Service file, Patchogue, NY.

Bury, R. B., and M. G. Raphael. 1983. Inventory methods for amphibians and reptiles. *In* J. F. Bell and T. Atterbury (eds.), Renewable Resources Inventories for Monitoring Changes and Trends, pp. 416-419. Oregon State University. Corvallis, OR.

Butterfield, B. P., M. J. Lanoo, and P. Nanjappa. 2005. *Rana spenocephala*. pages 586-587 *in* M. J. Lanoo, ed., Amphibian Declines; The Conservation Status of United States Species. University of California Press. Berkeley, CA.

Cagle, F. R. 1939. A system of marking turtles for future identification. Copeia 1939:170-173.

Caldecutt, W. J. 1997. Freshwater wetlands delineation and inventory of wetland herpetological species on Fire Island National Seashore. National Park Service. Patchogue, NY.

Conant, R. and J. T. Collins. 1998. A Field Guide to Reptile and Amphibians: Eastern and Central North America. 3rd Edition Expanded. Houghton Mifflin Co. Boston. MA.

Congdon, J. D., G. L. Breitenbach, R. C. van Loben Sels, and D. W. Tinkle. 1987. Reproduction and nesting ecology of snapping turtles (*Chelydra serpentina*) in southeastern Michigan. Herpetologica 43: 39-54.

Congdon, J. D., S. W. Gotte, and R. W. McDiarmid. 1992. Ontogenetic changes in habitat use by juvenile turtles, *Chelydra serpentina* and *Chrysemys picta*. Canadian Field Naturalist 106:241-248.

Connor, P. F. 1971. The mammals of Long Island, New York. NY State Museum Bulletin 416.

Cook, R. P. in prep. Amphibians and reptiles of Gateway NRA: Impacts of urbanization and restoration. Technical Report NPS/NER/NRTR-XXXX/xxx. National Park Service, Boston, MA.

Cook, R. P. 1989. A natural history of the diamondback terrapin. Underwater Naturalist 18:25-31.

Cook, R. P. 1996. Movement and ecology of eastern box and painted turtles repatriated to human-created habitat. PhD disseration, City University of New York.

Cook, R. P., K. M. Boland, S. J. Kot, J. Borgmeyer, and M. Schult. 2007. Inventory of aquatic turtles at Cape Cod National Seashore with recommendations for long term monitoring. Technical Report NPS/NER/NRTR-2007/091. National Park Service, Boston, MA.

Crother, B. I. (ED.). 2000. Scientific and Standard English Names of Amphibians and Reptiles of North America North of Mexico, with Comments Regarding Confidence in Our Understanding. Committee on Standard English and Scientific Names. Society for the Study of Amphibians and Reptiles Herpetological Circular No. 29. .

Crother, B. I., J. Boundy, J. A. Campbell, K. De Quieroz, D. Frost, D. M.Green, R. Highton, J. B. Iverson, R. W. McDiarmid, P. A. Meylan, T. W. Reeder, M. E. Seidel, J. W. Sites Jr., S. G. Tilley, and D. B. Wake. 2003. Scientific and Standard English Names of Amphibians and Reptiles of North America North of Mexico: Update. Herpetological Review 34:196–203.

Crouch, W. B. and P. W. C. Paton. 2002. Assessing the use of call surveys to monitor breeding anurans in Rhode Island. Journal of Herpetology 36:185-192.

Crump, M. L. and N. J.Scott.1994. Visual Encounter Surveys. *In* Heyer, R. W., M. A. Donnelly, R. W. McDiarmid, L. C. Hayek, M. S. Foster. 1994. Measuring and Monitoring Biological Diversity – Standard Methods for Amphibians. Pp 84-92. Smithsonian Institution Press. Washington, DC.

Daszak, P., L. Berger, A. A. Cunningham, A. D. Hyatt, D. E. Green, & R. Speare. 2000. Emerging Infectious Diseases and Amphibian Population Declines. Center for Disease Control. Vol. 5, No. 6.

Ditmars, R. L. 1896. The snakes found within fifty miles of New York City. Abstract of Proceedings of the Linnaean Society of New York 8:9-24.

Ditmars, R. L. 1905. The batrachians of the vicinity of New York City. Guide Leaflet Series No. 20, American Museum of Natural History. New York, NY.

Dodd, C. K. 2001. North American Box Turtles: A Natural History. Univ. of Oklahoma Press. Norman, OK.

Donaldson, B. M. and A. C. Echternacht. 2005. Aquatic habitat use relative to home range and seasonal movement of eastern box turtles (*Terrapene carolina carolina*: Emydidae) in eastern Tennessee. Journal of Herpetology 39:284-287.

Dunson, W. A., R. L. Wyman, and E. S. Corbett. 1992. A symposium on amphibian declines and habitat acidification. Journal of Herpetology 26:349-352.

Engelhardt, G. P. 1913. The reptiles of Long Island. Museum News 8:128-129.

Engelhardt, G. P., J. T. Nichols, R. Latham, and R. C. Murphy. 1915. Long Island Snakes. Copeia 17:1-4.

Ernst, C. H., J. E. Lovich, and R. W. Barbour. 1994. Turtles of the United States and Canada. Smithsonian Institution Press. Washington, DC.

Ernst, C. H. and E. M. Ernst. 2003. Snakes of the United States and Canada. Smithsonian Institution Press. Washington, DC.

Feinberg, J. A., and R. L. Burke. 2003. Nesting ecology and predation of diamondback terrapins, *Malaclemys terrapin*, at Gateway National Recreation Area, New York. Journal of Herpetology 37: 517-526.

Feinberg, J. A., J. Burger, and T. M. Green. 2007. The decline of southern leopard frogs from Long Island: Investigating causes and conservation strategies. Grant proposal to New York State Biodiversity Research Institute. www.nysm.nysed.gov/bri/grants/fy2007_2008/Abstract_Feinberg.pdf

Flora, M., G. Rosenlieb, C. Roman, and J. Ebert. 1992. Fire Island National Seashore Water Resources Scoping Report. National Park Service, Water Resources Div., Fort Collins, CO. Technical Report NPSINRWRDINRTR-92-11.

Frazer, N. B., J. W. Gibbons, and J. L. Greene. 1991. Life history and demography of the common mud turtle *Kinosternon subrubrum* in South Carolina, USA. Ecology 72:2218-2231.

Gibbs, J. P., A. R. Breisch, P .K. Ducey, G. Johnson, J. L Behler, and R. C. Bothner. 2007. The amphibians and reptiles of New York State. Oxford University Press. New York, NY.

Gibbons, J. W., and J. W. Coker 1978. Herpetofaunal colonization patterns of Atlantic coast barrier islands. American Midland Naturalist 99:219-233.

Golet, W. J. and T .A. Haines. 2001. Snapping turtles (*Chelydra serpentina*) as monitors for mercury contamination of aquatic environments. Environmental Monitoring and Assessment 71:211-220.

Graham, T. E. 1995. Habitat use and population parameters of the spotted turtle, *Clemmys guttata*, a species of special concern in Massachusetts. Chelonian Conservation and Biology 1: 207-214.

Graham, T. E., and V. H. Hutchison. 1969. Centenarian box turtles. International Turtle and Tortoise Society Journal 3(3):25-29.

Grant, B. W., A. D. Tucker, J. E. Lovich, A. M. Mills, P. M. Dixon and J. W. Gibbons. 1992. The use of coverboards in estimating patterns of reptile and amphibian biodiversity. *In* D. R. McCullough and R. H. Barrett (eds.). Wildlife 2001: Populations, pp. 379-403. Elsevier Science Publication. London, England.

Guillette, L. J., Jr. 2000. Contaminant-associated endocrine disruption in reptiles. *In* D. W. Sparling, G. Linder, and C. A. Bishop (eds.), Ecotoxicology of amphibians and reptiles, pp. 595-615. SETAC Press. Pensacola, FL.

Hall, R. J. 1980. Effects of environmental contaminants on reptiles: a review. United States Department of the Interior, Fish and Wildlife Service. Special Scientific Report – Wildlife Number 228. Washington, DC.

Harless, M., and H. Morlock. 1989. Turtles: Perspectives and Research. Robert E. Krieger Publishing Company. Malabar, FL 695pp.

Henry, F. P. H. 2000. Aspects of amphibian anatomy and physiology. *In* D. W. Sparling, G. Linder, and C. A. Bishop (eds.), Ecotoxicology of amphibians and reptiles, pp. 71-110. SETAC Press. Pensacola, FL.

Heyer, R. W., M. A. Donnelly, R. W. McDiarmid, L. C. Hayek, M. S. Foster. 1994. Measuring and Monitoring Biological Diversity – Standard Methods for Amphibians. Smithsonian Institution Press. Washington, DC.

Hunter, M. L., Calhoun, A. J. K., and M. McCollough. 1999. Maine Amphibians and Reptiles. University of Maine Press. Orono, ME 252pp.

Jankowski, P. 2004. An assessment of contaminant threats at Fire Island National Seashore DRAFT. Rutgers University School of Public Health.

Kieran, J. 1959. Natural History of New York City. Houghton-Mifflin Co. Boston, MA.

Kjoss, V. A. and J. A. Litvaitis. 2001. Community structure of snakes in a human-dominated landscape. Biological Conservation 98: 285-292.

Klemens, M. W. 1985. Survivors in megalopolis: Reptiles of the urban Northeast. Discovery 18:22-25.

Klemens, M. W. 1993. Amphibians and reptiles of Connecticut and adjacent regions. State Geological and Natural History Survey of Connecticut, Bulletin 112.

Klemens, M. W. 1997. Fire Island National Seashore, Sailor's Haven Field Notes. 7 July 1997. American Museum of Natural History Archive. Museum specimen AMNH 159078. New York, NY page 92.

Knapp, R. A., and K. R. Matthews. 2000. Non-native fish introductions and the decline of the Mountain Yellow-legged Frog from within protected areas. Conservation Biology 14:428-438.

Kroenke, A. E., E. L. Shuster, R. F .Bopp, and M .D. Gastrich. 2003. Assessment of historical and current trends in mercury deposition to New Jersey aquatic systems through analysis of sediment/soil cores. Research Summary. New Jersey Department of Environmental Protection, Division of Science, Research, and Technology. Trenton, NJ.

Kupferberg. S. 1994. Bullfrogs (*Rana catesbeiana*) invade a northern California watershed: impact on native frogs and hydrologic factors affecting establishment. American Zoologist 34:8A.

Lacki, M. J., J. W. Hummer, and H. J. Webster. 1992. Mine-drainage treatment wetland as habitat for herpetofaunal wildlife. Environmental Management 16:513-520.

Lazell, J. D. 1976. This Broken Archipelago. Demeter Press (Quadrangle, The New York Times Book Co). New York, NY.

Leng, C. W. and W. T. Davis. 1930. Staten Island and its people: A history. 1609-1929. Lewis Historical Publishing Company. New York, NY.

Mahmoud, I. Y. 1969. Comparative ecology of the Kinosternid turtles of Oklahoma. Southwestern Naturalist 14:31-66.

Mathewson, R. F. 1955. Reptiles and amphibians of Staten Island. Proceedings of the Staten Island Institute of Arts and Sciences Vol. XVIII: No.2.

McCormick, J. 1975. Environmental Inventory of the Fire Island National Seashore. Jack McCormick and Associates, Devon, PA.

Meyer, M. E. 1988. Investigating the eastern mud turtle (*Kinosternon subrubrum subrubrum*). New York State Department of Environmental Conservation. Stony Brook, NY.

Meylan, A., and S. Sadove. 1986. Cold-stunning in Long Island Sound, New York. Marine Turtle Newsletter (37):7-8.

Mitchell, J. C., and J. M. Anderson. 1994. Amphibians and Reptiles of Assateague and Chincoteague Islands. Virginia Museum of Natural History. Martinsville, VA.

Mitchell, J. C. ,and M. W. Klemens. 2000. Primary and secondary effects of habitat alteration. In: Turtle Conservation, p. 5-32. Klemens, M. W., Ed, Smithsonian Institution Press. Washington, DC.

Morreale, S. J., A. B. Meylan, S. S. Sadove, and E. A. Standora. 1992. Annual occurrence and winter mortality of marine turtles in New York waters. Journal of Herpetology 26:301-308.

Murphy, R. C. 1916. Long Island Turtles. Copeia 33:56-60.

Murphy, R. C. 1950. August on Fire Island Beach. Science Guide No. 134, American Museum of Natural History, New York, NY.

National Park Service. 2000. Strategic Plan for Fire Island National Seashore. Fiscal Year 2001 to 2005. National Park Service. Patchogue, NY. http://www.nps.gov/fiis/stratplanFY01-05.htm

New York State Department of Environmental Conservation. 2000. Endangered Species
    Program. http://www.dec.state.ny.us/website/dfwmr/wildlife/endspec/

New York State Department of Environmental Conservation. 2008. Hydrogen ion concentration
    as pH (2006). Acid Deposition Monitoring Program.
    http://www.dec.ny.gov/chemical/38884.html

Nichols, J. T. 1914. Mud turtle attacked by crab. Copeia 12:3.

Nichols, J. T. 1939. Data on size, growth, and age in the box turtle, Terrapene carolina. Copeia
    1939(1):14-20.

Nichols, J. T. 1947. Notes on the mud turtle. Herpetologica 3:147-148.

Noble, G. K. 1926. The Long Island newt: a contribution to the life history of *Triturus
    viridescens*. Amererican Museum Novitates 228:l-11.

Noble, G. K. 1927. Distributional list of the reptiles and amphibians of the New York City region.
    Guide Leaflet Series No.69, American Museum of Natural History. New York, NY.

Northup, J. G. 1986. A progress report on the ecological inventory project-Fire Island
    National Seashore. National Park Service. Patchogue, NY.

Oliver, J. A. 1955. The natural history of North American amphibians and reptiles.
    D. Van Nostrand Company. Princeton, NJ.

Overton, F. 1914. Long Island flora and fauna III: the frogs and toads (Order Salientia). Museum
    of the Brooklyn Institute of Arts and Science, Science Bulletin 2(3):21-40.

Pough, F. H., and M. B. Pough. 1968. The systematic status of painted turtles (*Chrysemys*) in
    the northeastern United States. Copeia 1968:612-618.

Putnam, J. 1999. A search for the Eastern Hognose Snake (*Heterodon platyrhinos*) at
    Fire Island National Seashore, Final Report. National Park Service. Patchogue, NY.

Psuty, N. P., M. Grace, and J. P. Pace. 2005. The Coastal Geomorphology of Fire
    Island: A Portrait of Continuity and Change (Fire Island National Seashore Science
    Synthesis Paper). Technical Report NPS/NER/NRTR—2005/021. National Park Service.
    Boston, MA.

Reagan D. P. 1974. Habitat selection in the three-toed box turtle, *Terrapene carolina triunguis*.
    Copeia 1974: 512-527.

Rozsa, R. 1972. Checklist to the invertebrates, fish, amphibians and mammals of the Fire Island
    National Seashore. National Park Service. Patchogue, NY (mimeo). Cited by McCormick
    1975 and Northup 1986.

Schlauch, F. C. 1976. City snakes, suburban salamanders. Natural History 85:46-53.

Schlauch, F. C. 1978. Urban geographical ecology of the amphibians and reptiles of Long Island. In C.M. Kirkpatrick (ed.), Wildlife and People, pp. 25-41. John S. Wright Forestry Conference Proceedings, Cooperative Extension Service, Purdue University. West Lafayette, IN.

Shoop, C. R. and R. D. Kenney. 1992. Seasonal distribution and abundance of loggerhead and leatherback sea turtles in waters of the northeastern United States. Herpetological Monographs 6:43-67.

Smith, E. 1899. The turtles and lizards found in the vicinity of New York City. Abstract of Proceedings of the Linnaean Society of New York 11: 11-32.

Smith, J. D. 1962. Land turtles on Fire Island. Long Island Forum. Vol. 25, No. 1. pp. 9, 21-22.

Smith, J. D. 1963. Puff adders. Long Island Forum. Vol. 26, No. 8. pp. 185-186.

Stickel, L. F. 1951. Wood mouse and box turtle populations in an area treated annually with DDT for five years. Journal of Wildlife Management 15(2):161-164.

Stumpel, A. H. P. 1992. Successful reproduction of introduced bullfrogs *Rana catesbeiana* in northwestern Europe: a potential threat to indigenous amphibians. Biological Conservation 60:61-62.

Trapido, H. 1937. The snakes of New Jersey, A guide. The Newark Museum. Newark NJ.

Tupper, T. A. and R. P.Cook. 2008. Habitat variables influencing breeding effort in northern clade *Bufo fowleri*: Implications for conservation. Applied Herpetology 5:101-119.

Tupper, T. A., R. P. Cook, B. C. Timm, and A. Goodstine. 2007. Improving call surveys for detecting Fowler's toad, *Bufo fowleri*, in Southern New England, USA. Applied Herpetology 4:245-259.

Unrine, J. M., C. H. Jagoe, W. A. Hopkins, and H. A. Brant. 2004. Adverse effects of ecologically relevant dietary mercury exposure in southern leopard frog (*Rana sphenocephala*) larvae. Environmental Toxicology and Chemistry. 23:2964-2970.

Williamson, L. 1999. FIIS I&M Data Report. Fire Island National Seashore. Patchogue, NY.

Wood, R. C., and R. Herlands. 1997. Turtles and tires: The impact of roadkills on Northern Diamondback Terrapin, *Malaclemys terrapin terrapin*, populations on the Cape May peninsiula, southern New Jersey, USA. In: Proceedings: Conservation, Restoration, and Management of Tortoises and Turtles–an International Conference, p. 46-53i. Van Abbema, J. Ed., New York Turtle and Tortoise Society. New York, NY

Yeaton, S. C. 1968. The amphibia of Long Island. Sanctuary 1968 Summer:2-19. The Nature Conservancy. Cold Spring Harbor, NY.

Yeaton, S. C.1972. A natural history of Long Island. The Nature Conservancy. Cold Spring Harbor, NY.

Personal Communications

Feinberg, Jeremy. Department of Ecology, Evolution, and Natural Resources, Rutgers University, New Brunswick, NJ (PhD student)

Finn, Steve. Fire Island National Seashore, Patchogue NY (former employee)

Lamont, MaryLaura, Fire Island National Seashore, Patchogue NY

Psuty, Norbert. Institute of Marine and Coastal Sciences, Rutgers, The State University of New Jersey, Sandy Hook, NJ 07732

Rozsa, Ronald. Fire Island National Seashore, Patchogue NY (former employee)

Soule, Norm. Director, Cold Spring Harbor Fish Hatchery, Cold Spring Harbor, NY

Stavdal, Richard. Fire Island National Seashore, Patchogue NY (former employee)

Appendix A. Prior records of amphibians and reptiles on Fire Island National Seashore.

Sea turtle species are migrants. All others are resident. *NY=New York, F=Federal. SC=Special Concern, T=Threatened, E=Endangered. American bullfrog is likely a recent arrival at FIIS.

SPECIES (CONSERVATION LISTING)*	Overton (1914)	Murphy (1950)	Smith (1962)	Smith (1963)	Yeaton (1974)	Northup (1986)	Meyer (1988)	Morreale et al. (1992)	Barcia (1996)	Caldecutt (1997)	Klemens (1997)	Putnam (1999)	Williamson (1999)	NYDEC (2000)
Fowler's toad		X				X				X	X	X		
Southern leopard frog	X													
American bullfrog (Recent Arrival)												X		
Snapping turtle							X		X	X		X		
Eastern box turtle NY(SC)			X			X			X	X		X		
Northern diamond-backed terrapin						X	X		X	X		X	X	
Spotted turtle NY(SC)						X			X	X		X		
Eastern mud turtle NY(E)							X		X	X				
Loggerhead sea turtle NY&F(T)														X
Green sea turtle NY&F(T)								X						
Leatherback sea turtle NY&F(E)														X
Northern black racer		X				X				X		X		
Eastern garter snake										X		X		
Eastern hog-nosed snake NY(SC)		X		X	X									

91

Appendix B. Habitat Categories.

	Habitat Type	Description
	tidal marsh/swamp	Bayside, brackish, open habitat with a network of mosquito ditches throughout. Dense stands of herbaceous wetland vegetation subject to changes in water depth during each tidal cycle. Swamp areas with low shrubs, *Phragmites*, and briar thickets (*Smilax* spp.) occur along the interior margins of the marsh.
	non-tidal marsh	Fresh or slightly brackish body of water without well-defined borders, supporting abundant vegetation such as deciduous trees (e.g., red maple (*Acer rubrum*)), shrubs (e.g., buttonbush (*Cephalanthus occidentalis*), bayberry (*Myrica cerifera*)), and emergent, herbaceous vegetation (e.g., soft rush (*Juncus effuses*); sedges (*Carex* spp.)). Water is usually shallow (<1m) and substrate mucky.
Wetland	permanent pond	Open body of water (<2 ha), holds water the entire year, and fish are usually present. Borders of the pond are well defined.
	temporary pond	Open or closed canopy body of water that holds water for part of the year, drying during summer months, and is void of fish. Identified by water stained leaves and buttressed tree trunks (e.g., pin oak (*Quercus palustris*); black gum (*Nyssa sylvatica*)). Invertebrates present include fairy shrimp, predacious diving beetles, copepods, cladocerans, and caddisfly larvae.
	holly/mixed forest	Closed canopy forest dominated by holly (*Ilex opaca*). Other species include black gum (*Nyssa sylvatica*), red maple (*Acer rubrum*), and pine (*Pinus* spp.). Temporary freshwater ponds are found interspersed throughout the forest while non-tidal marsh habitats dominated by *Phragmites* are found along the bayside margins of the forest.
Upland	beachgrass/beach heather/low thicket	A mixture of bare sand, low herbaceous vegetation (beachgrass *Ammophila breviligulata*, beach heather *Hudsonia tomentosa*), and shrubs (bayberry *Myrica pennsylvanica*) less than four feet.
	developed	Private residential community with trails, roads, managed lawns, buildings and small open sandy or vegetated areas.

93

Appendix C. GPS positions for 30 standardized survey sites and 11 incidental encounter locations on Fire Island National Seashore.

2002-2003. UTM meters, Zone 18N, NAD 1983.

Standardized Survey Sites	UTM X	UTM Y	UTM X	UTM Y
Bellport Bay	676403	4509691		
Bigfoot Pond	677146	4509932		
Carrington Swamp				
Hospital Point Cranberry Bog	678332	4510537		
Hospital Point Ditches	677924	4510712		
Kismet Bayside				
Kismet Interior				
Kismet Pond	651536	4499782		
Molasses Point Ditches	675165	4509316		
Molasses Point Marsh	674963	4509086		
Old Inlet to Bellport Beach (bayside)	675165	4509316	677690	4510395
Old Inlet to Bellport Beach (interior)	675200	4508960	677714	4510341
Sailor's Haven Maintenance Pond	660375	4502409		
Sailor's Haven Bayside	659456	4502329	660123	4502381
Sailor's Haven Interior	660506	4502447	660544	4502403
Sedge Meadow east Kismet Pond	651595	4499790		
Smith Point to Old Inlet (bayside)	680020	4511646	677686	4510410
Smith Point to Old Inlet (interior)	680004	4511424	680138	4511206
Sunken Forest	659435	4502267		
Sunken Forest Pond 2	659491	4502205		
Sunken Forest Pond 4	659543	4502264		
Sunken Forest Pond 6	659659	4502242		
Sunken Forest Pond 7	659762	4502237		
Sunken Forest Pond 8	659898	4502289		
Transect 4 Marsh	678499	4510539		
Watch Hill Bayside	670914	4507103	670145	4506751
Watch Hill Boardwalk Pond	670035	4506402		
Watch Hill Ditches	670145	4506751	670194	4506618
Watch Hill Interior	670969	4506859	670979	4506818
Watch Hill Pond 12-37	670077	4506458		

Appendix C (continued).

Incidental Encounter Locations	UTM X	UTM Y	UTM X	UTM Y
Lonelyville	654200	4500565		
Ocean Bay Park	657171	4501416		
Ocean Beach	657356	4501276		
Old Inlet	677751	4510262		
Otis Pike Wilderness Area (OPWA)				
Point O'Woods	657814	4501674		
Sailor's Haven	659928	4502218		
Saltaire	652284	4499873		
Sunken Forest Carex Marsh	659264	4502182		
Sunken Forest Pond 5	659604	4502266		
Watch Hill	669990	4506421		

Appendix D. Measurements of turtles captured on Fire Island National Seashore in 2002 and 2003.

Species	Date	Site	Notch Code	Carapace Length (mm)	Carapace Width (mm)	Plastron Length (mm)	Weight (g)	Sex	Age Category
Snapping turtle	4/12/2002	Kismet Pond	L10	300.4	245.7	213.4	6250	male	adult
	4/15/2002	Kismet Pond	L11	118.4	98.3	87.8	345	male	juvenile
	5/1/2002	Kismet Pond	R11	267	236	198.9	4500	female	adult
	5/1/2002	Sunken Forest Pond 2	R12	92.1	76.3	65.0	169	female	juvenile
	5/1/2002	Watch Hill Boardwalk Pond		60.3	48.9	43.0	49	female	juvenile
	5/2/2002	Kismet Pond	R10	284	227	203.0	4600	male	adult
	5/3/2002	Sunken Forest Pond 7	R10	87.4	70.7	63.0	139	female	juvenile
	5/27/2002	Kismet Pond	L12	178.7	151.8	131.7	1220	male	juvenile
	5/27/2002	Sunken Forest Pond 4	R9	206.6	158.9	147.1	1740	male	juvenile
	5/27/2002	Sunken Forest Pond 6	L9	206.9	192	159.4	2010	male	juvenile
	5/28/2002	Kismet Pond	R10, L10	402	344	250.0	14500	male	adult
	5/28/2002	Kismet Pond	R11, L11	289.4	245.9	202.9	5000	male	adult
	5/29/2002	Kismet Pond	R11, L10	312	256.5	220.4	no data	male	adult
	5/31/2002	Sunken Forest Pond 4	R10,L11	112.3	88.9	80.3	305	female	juvenile
	6/5/2002	Kismet Pond		50.7	44.5	34.5	31	unknown	juvenile
	6/11/2002	Kismet Pond	R9, L9	53.8	47.7	38.2	37.5	unknown	juvenile
	6/12/2002	Kismet Pond	R10, L10	59.6	49.3	40.7	43	unknown	juvenile
	6/21/2002	Watch Hill Boardwalk	L10	62	52.4	43.9	53	unknown	juvenile
	7/29/2002	SH Maintenance Pond	R10 L9	212.2	176.2	154.3	2000	male	adult
	8/27/2002	SH Maintenance Pond	R8	218	171.3	148.4	2200	female	adult
	8/27/2002	SH Maintenance Pond	R11 L9	255	199	166.0	3500	male	adult
	5/27/2003	Bellport Bay/ Old Inlet Ditches	R10	145.4	118.5	103.0	640	male	juvenile

97

Species	Date	Site	Notch Code	Carapace Length (mm)	Carapace Width (mm)	Plastron Length (mm)	Weight (g)	Sex	Age Category
Spotted turtle	5/29/2003	Transect 4 Marsh	R9	78	64.4	50.3	118	juvenile	juvenile
	4/30/2002	Watch Hill Pond 37		ESCAPED			122	Male	adult
	4/30/2002	Watch Hill Pond 37	R1	102	80	91.9	158	male	adult
	5/1/2002	Watch Hill Pond 37	R2	100.7	77.5	92.0	145	female	adult
	5/2/2002	Watch Hill Pond 37	R1,2	104.3	79.0	92.1	167	female	adult
	5/3/2002	Watch Hill Pond 37	R3	105	78.1	92.1	150	male	adult
	6/21/2002	Watch Hill Boardwalk	R2,3	103	76.7	95.3	89.5	female	adult
	6/21/2002	Watch Hill Boardwalk	R1,3	94.6	75.6	89.8	72	female	adult
Eastern mud turtle	6/7/2002	Bigfoot Pond	R1	90	65.5	78.3	130	male	adult
	5/19/2003	Transect 4 Marsh	R9	40.2	36.5	37.0	15.5	unknown	juvenile
	5/20/2003	Transect 4 Marsh	R2	86.6	63.3	no data	130	male	adult
	5/21/2003	Bigfoot Pond	R1,2	93.4	68.6	84.2	150	male	adult
	5/212003	Bigfoot Pond	R3	88	66.2	no data	136	female	adult
	5/21/03	Bigfoot Pond	R1	RECAP FROM 6/7/2002			138	Male	adult
	5/28/2003	Bellport Bay/ Old Inlet Ditches	L2	49.1	39.8	no data	23	unknown	juvenile
	5/28/2003	Bigfoot Pond	L1	84.8	68	56.6	128	female	adult
	5/29/2003	Bellport Bay/ Old Inlet Ditches	R2,3	54.1	44.2	no data	31	female	juvenile
	5/30/2003	Bellport Bay/ Old Inlet Ditches	R8	83.8	65.1	no data	127	female	adult
	5/31/2003	Bellport Bay/ Old Inlet Ditches	R1,3	59.4	47.3	no data	41	female	juvenile
	6/2/2003	Transect 4 Marsh	R2,8	74	59.1	no data	82	female	juvenile
	6/2/2003	Transect 4 Marsh	L4	97.2	74	94.7	181	female	adult

Species	Date	Site	Notch Code	Carapace Length (mm)	Carapace Width (mm)	Plastron Length (mm)	Weight (g)	Sex	Age Category
Northern diamond-backed terrapin	6/5/2002	Bellport Bay/ Old Inlet Ditches	R2	210.3	162	194.3	1510	female	adult
	6/5/2002	Smith Point to Old Inlet Interior (Burma Road)	R11	182	132.9	168.6	860	female	adult
	6/7/2002	Smith Point to Old Inlet Interior (Burma Road at Transect 4 Marsh)		29.4	26.2	24.6	6.5	unknown	juvenile
Eastern box turtle	5/30/2002	Sunken Forest Pond 7	R2	134.2	103.1	128.9	500	female	adult
	6/19/2002	Old Kismet Fire Station	R2	83.9	66	no data	120	unknown	juvenile
	6/24/2002	Sunken Forest Pond 7	R3	158.7	117.1	no data	615	male	adult
	6/24/2002	VES Sunken Forest	R9	121.4	96.4	no data	425	female	adult
	6/24/2002	VES Sunken Forest	R1,2	120	90.5	no data	252	unknown	juvenile
	6/24/2002	VES Sunken Forest	R1	127.3	104.8	126.3	440	male	adult
	8/27/2002	Sunken Forest Pond 4	R1,8	141.6	110.2	no data	590	female	adult
	8/27/2002	Sunken Forest Pond 5	R1,2,4	141.3	111.2	no data	550	male	adult
	8/27/2002	Sunken Forest Pond 7	R2,4	139.7	113	133.4	500	male	adult
	8/27/2002	VES Sunken Forest	R2,3	142.8	119.1	no data	420	male	adult
	8/27/2002	VES Sunken Forest	R1,3	135	109.5	no data	470	male	adult
	8/27/2002	VES Sunken Forest	R4	161.7	123.9	154.2	660	male	adult
	8/27/2002	VES Sunken Forest	R1,4	144.5	114.7	137.5	470	male	adult
	8/29/2002	Ocean Bay Park	R2,8	150.4	115.7	143.7	550	male	adult
	8/29/2002	Sunken Forest Pond 8	R1,2,8	114.6	89.7	113.4	266	female	juvenile
	9/3/2002	Point O Woods	R3,8	141.8	114.7	136.5	560	male	adult
	9/15/2002	Kismet Beach	R11	152	117.1	143.3	555	male	adult

Appendix E. Measurements of snakes captured on Fire Island National Seashore, 2002.

Species	Date	Site	Method of Capture	Sex	Snout Vent Length (mm)	Total Length (mm)	Weight (g)
	6/4/2002	Old Inlet to Bellport Beach (interior)	Incidental	male	1004	1239	480
	6/3/2002	Old Inlet to Bellport Beach (interior)	Incidental	male	914	1225	375
	6/3/2002	Old Inlet to Bellport Beach (interior)	Incidental	female	1234	1544	770
	8/14/2002	Kismet Interior-Fire Station	Incidental	juvenile	260	340	7
	6/3/2002	Old Inlet to Bellport Beach (interior)- CB Array 4	Coverboard	male	280	362	8
Northern black racer	5/7/2002	Smith Point to Old Inlet Interior	VES	male	925	1235	286
	4/10/2002	Smith Point to Old Inlet Interior	VES	male	252	316	6.5
	8/12/2002	Kismet Interior- Ranger Check Station	Incidental	female	1250	1600	880
	4/30/2002	Sunken Forest Pond 7 East	Incidental	male	1130	1420	580
	4/30/2002	Sunken Forest Pond 7 East	Incidental	male	1188	1473	775
	8/29/2002	Sailor's Haven Interior CB Array 1	Coverboard	female	650	910	156
	6/21/2002	Watch Hill	Incidental	male	1050	1350	380
Eastern garter snake	6/6/2002	Kismet Pond	Incidental	male	491	580	52
	8/5/2002	Kismet Interior- Ranger Check Station	Incidental	female	690	863	123

NPS 615/105745, September 2010